EFFECTIVE PROBLEM SOLVING$_{C \cdot 1}$

Marvin Levine

State University of New York at Stony Brook

Prentice Hall

Englewood Cliffs, New Jersey 07632

Library of Congress Cataloging-in-Publication Data

Levine, Marvin, 1928-
    Effective problem solving.

    Bibliography: p.
    Includes index.
    1. Problem solving. I. Title.
QA63.L48 1988   153.4'3   87-17444
ISBN 0-13-244823-8

Editorial/production supervision and
    interior design: Carole Brown and Barbara Marttine
Cover design: Photo Plus Art
Manufacturing buyer: Ray Keating

Printed in the United States of America

10 9 8 7 6 5 4 3 2 1

ISBN 0-13-244823-8 01

Prentice-Hall International (UK) Limited, *London*
Prentice-Hall of Australia Pty. Limited, *Sydney*
Prentice-Hall Canada Inc., *Toronto*
Prentice-Hall Hispanoamericana, S.A., *Mexico*
Prentice-Hall of India Private Limited, *New Delhi*
Prentice-Hall of Japan, Inc., *Tokyo*
Simon & Schuster Asia Pte. Ltd., *Singapore*
Editora Prentice-Hall do Brasil, Ltda., *Rio de Janeiro*

For my beloved Tillie, who, as these pages were going to press, posed the ultimate insoluble problem

CONTENTS

PREFACE

Why another book on how to solve problems? What will this book contribute to an already large literature?

To answer these questions we need a brief overview of the existing literature as well as some analysis of what is meant by such phrases as heuristics, or prescriptive rules (the label that I prefer), or principles of effective problem solving. First, much of the how-to-solve-problems literature is restricted to a particular class of problems. Thus, there is one set of books on how to solve mathematics and engineering problems, another set on solving poorly defined problems, typically slanted toward industrial needs, and a third set on problems involving other people. This book differs from these restricted texts in that it draws from all these sources. In addition, these three domains are supplemented with other topics: problems of appliance repair, comprehension, and remembering. Thus, unlike most of the books dealing with problem-solving principles, this book is a survey, covering a variety of topics.

Of course, this work is not alone in providing a survey. Even after eliminating the specialized problem-solving texts, a few remain that have a breadth comparable to this one. Compared to these, however, this book has several unique, noteworthy features:

1. It makes explicit the distinction, first applied by Scriven (1980) to problem solving, between descriptive principles (how one does solve problems) and prescriptive principles (how one *should* solve problems). Authors generally have ignored the distinction and have blurred or even confused the two. To take some common examples, most books describe hill climbing and means–ends analysis as problem-solving strategies. It is never made clear, however, whether these are descriptive rules, that is, strategies that people routinely apply, for better or for worse, or prescriptive rules, that is, the best possible strategies. Chapters on logical thinking typically tell us about the errors people make (descriptive) in logic problems but never tell us what one should do, what specific techniques one might invoke (prescriptive), to avoid these errors.

   I, by contrast, have tried to hold consistently to this distinction. This book is organized around prescriptive principles; it offers a collection of specific procedures that one should employ for various classes of problems. A good metaphor for such principles is that of tools in a tool box. Just as different tools are appropriate for different tasks, so are the various prescriptions presented here appropriate for different types of problems. And just as training in the use of saws, drills, and other tools will permit one to construct a wide variety of objects, so should training in prescriptive principles permit better handling of a wide variety of problems.

2. There is throughout a sensitivity to the range of abstractness of prescriptive principles. Prescriptive rules can, at one extreme, be concrete and specific (e.g., in geometry, "If you want to prove that two angles are equal, try to show that they are corresponding parts of congruent triangles."). Such rules are typically narrow in application—so narrow as to have little utility for enhancing general problem-solving skills. At the other extreme, prescriptive rules can be highly abstract and general (e.g., "The first step is to formulate a plan." Or simply, "Think!"). At this extreme we have no guide for how to proceed. As one reviewer of a recent book on problem solving noted: "the advice is a little like that frequently given to nervous people: 'What you've got to do is relax!' What the anxious and the puzzled both want to know is, how?" (Chance, 1985).

    In this book I have kept to a middle ground, describing principles that are of sufficient generality to have some breadth of applicability but with enough concreteness so that one can know how to proceed. Now and then I have veered toward the extremes but always consciously, always forcing myself to justify the inclusion of such principles.

3. Some principles recommended here go beyond those in the existing literature. Included are principles that I have informally detected during a long research career on problem solving. For example, the principles that come under the heading of *intimate engagement* deal in part with motivating oneself in a problem-solving situation. And the principle *take a problem-solving stance* deals with handling one's emotions during interpersonal problem solving. In the formal research literature the areas connecting motivation and emotion to problem solving are completely uncharted. Hence, they have been ignored by other authors. They are included here, however, despite this lack of a rigorous foundation. These principles are sufficiently important, and my own experiences provide, I think, sufficient face validity to warrant their inclusion.

4. Correspondingly, some of the topics discussed here go beyond those found in other problem-solving books. This is the only survey text that deals, for example, with appliance repair and with

problems that arise between people. It is remarkable that these topics should be omitted from all the other surveys of problem solving, but that is currently the case.

I believe, therefore, that this book has several advantages relative to those already on the market. The student who reads it carefully (or, as I prefer to say, engages it intimately) should, of course, be better able to deal with problems as they arise. An unexpected byproduct is that the student should acquire a deeper grasp of human nature. This latter claim is spelled out in the concluding chapter, but I want to make the reader aware of it and to justify it here. The realization thrust itself upon me as I was completing the work and began to see the overall pattern. Most of the principles that I present are concerned with how we can overcome our own limitations in trying to solve a problem. Thus, I review our cognitive-resource limitations, the inhibitions that prevent us from confronting a problem, the emotions, particularly in interpersonal problems, that prevent our finding sensible solutions, the functional blindness that we call *einstellung*, and more. Wherever appropriate, these limitations are described and prescriptive principles are presented as attempts to overcome these limitations. The student, thus, can learn not only principles for dealing with problems but also what it is about ourselves that can make the problem more or less difficult.

I have written this book for college freshmen and sophomores, and for students who have not yet had a course that reviews cognitive psychology. As such, enjoyment of the book is not dependent upon knowledge from other texts. Nevertheless, the ideal use would be as a supplementary text in courses on critical thinking, cognition, or, of course, problem solving.

Many people suggested problems and examples that found their way into these pages. In this regard I would like to thank Phil Ball, Dave Emmerich, Don Lauer, Fred Levine, Ernie Odom, Mary Peterson, John Sweller, Stanley Thompson, and my family—Arthur, Laurie, Tillie, and Todd.

Marvin Levine

A WORD TO THE READER

It has been my aim to make this book instructive, helpful, and fun.

The book is *instructive* in revealing many things about human nature, that is, about ourselves—about our cognitive, motivational, and emotional limitations. These limitations not only impair our ability to solve the problems around us but may even be the cause of those problems.

The book is *helpful* in that it does more than simply describe these limitations. It provides a variety of concrete, specific proposals for surmounting these restrictions caused by our own human nature. By overcoming these inner obstacles, we become better problem solvers.

Finally, the book is *fun* precisely because it deals with problems and problem solving. There is the tantalizing challenge of logical puzzles, the delight in creative, roundabout solutions to everyday obstacles, and the intrinsic fascination in the drama of human problems. I dare say that you will not feel that you wasted your time reading this book.

In different sections of the book you will review principles for solving at least six different types of problems, from machines that need repairing, to mathematical puzzles, to difficulties between people. Some of you are already skilled in one or more of these areas. As a result, you may find some of these sections elementary, containing suggestions that are painfully obvious to you. Those of you who can take a car engine apart and put it back together will be amused at the simple nature of the proposals here for repairing things. Those of you who are habitually diplomatic and behave wisely in social situations will wonder why I bother to spell out what you already know. Nevertheless, there is enough variety in this book so that all of you should find something to learn. Be patient, then, should you find an occasional obvious analysis. Other sections will be more enlightening.

Throughout the text I have frequently presented an instruction (e.g., to try to solve a problem or to read and remember a particular passage) followed by a line of asterisks. You will make most effective use of this book if, at that point, you stop your reading and follow the instruction. This is an exercise in participant learning.

One final detail. I have an abiding interest in the experiences that people have in solving problems. It is my hope that after reading this book you will become more sensitive to the problem-solving processes within your own experience. If you encounter a problem for which you feel you produced a novel solution, I would be delighted to know about it. If you are willing to jot down a description of the problem, the solution, and the process by which you came to the solution, feel free to send it along to me. I would consider it a privilege.

Marvin Levine

Department of Psychology

State University of New York at Stony Brook

Stony Brook, N.Y. 11794

PRESCRIPTIVE
PRINCIPLES

1

DESCRIPTIVE
AND PRESCRIPTIVE
PRINCIPLES

The science of problem solving is unusual compared with other scientific domains. Certainly, it parallels—even imitates—the experimental and theoretical analyses of traditional science. In any experimental science the researcher brings the subject matter into the laboratory, studies it under various circumstances, and theorizes about those processes that cannot be directly observed. For example, the geneticist may study X-ray diffraction photographs and then theorize about gene structure; the astonomer studies spectrograms and then theorizes about the dynamics of the universe. Similarly, the problem-solving researcher brings the subject (for our purposes, the human adult) into the laboratory, presents a problem, and observes the behavior, that is, the efforts to solve the problem. Some aspects of the behavior (the time to solve, the type of errors made, etc.) constitute the data. Theoretical analysis is required by the fact that the problem-solving processes are unseen. These processes include strategies being used, hypotheses being tested, thoughts, imagery, and the like. They all take place within the head of the subject and are hidden from the scientist. The description of such processes is the task of theory. Like any scientist, then, the researcher on problem solving obtains relevant data and theorizes about hidden processes.

To put it another way, the researcher is trying to derive theoretical principles describing how people solve problems. We will call these *descriptive* principles of problem solving. In the search for descriptive principles the science of problem solving is like any other science.

What makes this particular science peculiar is that the scientist wants to know not only how people, in fact, do solve problems, but also how they *should* solve problems. Here we leave classical science. The physicist does not ask: How *should* the universe be organized? What *should* the gravitational constant be? The universe is expanding, the constant is 32 ft/sec^2, and that's that. In studying problem solving, however, we seek not only descriptions but prescriptions as well. What *should* one do to increase the likelihood of solving the problem? If there are traps in a given type of problem, what *should* one do to best avoid them? That is, we want a set of principles that tell not merely how people do behave in solving a problem, but how they should behave. We will call these *prescriptive* principles of problem solving, to distinguish them from the descriptive principles.

Descriptive principles of problem solving are well known within the field of psychology. They have been comprehensively reviewed in one recent textbook (Mayer, 1983), and partial reviews may be found in almost any text dealing with cognitive processes. There is no comparable review of prescriptive rules. These tend to be domain specific, with different authors characterizing different principles. To name a few examples, for mathematical problem solving we have the work of Polya (1957) and Wickelgren (1974). For organizational and engineering problem solving there is Osborne's (1963) work on brainstorming and de Bono's (1970) description of lateral thinking. Principles of interpersonal problem solving have been developed by clinical psychologists, especially by those concerned with social skills or assertiveness training. Thus, there is a wide mix of prescriptive principles.

One aim of this book, then, is to present something approaching a comprehensive statement of these prescriptive rules as I know them. This will include not only those principles that are scattered throughout the literature, but those that I myself have discovered and employed during a twenty-year career in the field of problem solving.

A secondary aim is to relate these prescriptive rules to current descriptive theory, wherever that is possible. It should be noted, however, that that will definitely be secondary. For the most part, the derivation of prescriptive principles from theory is beyond the state of the art. Where these are related to theory or research, the connection, of course, will be made explicit. But the absence of research, of even validating research, will not prevent consideration of principles that have face validity, that is, principles that seem sensible.

INTIMATE ENGAGEMENT

2

THE PRINCIPLE OF INTIMATE ENGAGEMENT (USE YOUR EYES)

For the most part, all descriptive and prescriptive principles of problem solving are cognitive. That is, the principles characterize the way in which the mind manipulates information. The prescriptive principle that we will consider first, *intimate engagement,* is different in that it has a motivational emphasis. As such, it has relevance to all problem solving. For this reason and for others that I will discuss later, it is probably the most valuable principle in this book.

During the war in Korea I was in the army, an eager corporal assigned to a psychology research laboratory. We soldiers assisted the civilian psychologists with their research programs. The project to which I was assigned investigated the problem of nighttime patrolling. According to the reports sent back from Korea, men assigned to infiltrate enemy lines at night for the purpose of obtaining information typically failed. They almost always reported finding or seeing nothing of interest. Our mission was to improve the information yielded by these nighttime patrols. The lab specifically studied training methods to improve both vision at night and map use.

One day a colonel, recently returned from combat, visited the laboratory and was briefed by the various project directors. One of my minor jobs was to chauffeur the VIPs, so I drove this colonel back to the officers' club. During the drive we talked about our project, patrolling at night. His comment (or words to this effect) was: "You guys are doing good things. Map reading, night vision. Yeah, we need to know about that. In my experience, though, the most important thing is the guy's 'guts.' He's got to be willing to get out there, past the enemy lines, and take the time to look around. Then you'll get your information."

Common sense said the colonel had to be right. It would be too easy for soldiers to go out into the darkness, to stop well beyond the view of their own lines but certainly before reaching the enemy lines, and to wait a couple of hours. They could then return saying they saw nothing. We were studying skills and perception (map reading and night vision) when the difficulty may well have been one of motivation. Whether the colonel was right or wrong, his comment impressed on me the relative importance of motivation—of the willingness to get out there and look—on problem solving.

How does the issue of motivation apply to problem solving in general? The soldiers, after all, may have failed to solve their problem of obtaining information, but they minimized the risk to their lives. How does motivation apply to problem solving, when such life-and-death stakes are not involved? The motivation is manifested in a more subtle way, but it is, nevertheless, evident. For a given type of problem (e.g., an appliance repair problem, a riddle, or math problem), people vary in their willingness to "engage" the problem. Try the following: Present your friends with the cryptarithmetic problem portrayed in Figure 2.1. Some will gaze at it for a minute, say something like, "I'm not very good at this," and dismiss the task. Others will stop whatever they were doing, take out a pencil, pore over every letter, and be lost to society for as long as it takes to solve. The latter have engaged the problem intimately; the former have not.

There is a plausible, descriptive explanation for the difference between these two extreme behaviors. The engager, it is said, has had a history of success with similar problems; the dismisser has had a history of failure. The dismisser, it would appear, is a captive of the past. Presumably, unless retrained with successes, the dismisser will always turn away.

I would suggest that that description is oversimplified. It leaves out of consideration the inner state of the problem solver. Puzzles, like most challenges, are intrinsically interesting, attractive, and tantalizing. After a history of failure, the threat of another failure posed by a puzzle produces a negative emotional attitude, a kind of low-level anxiety. This negative, inhibiting emotion outweighs the positive, attracting character of the puzzle. Thus, a history of failure changes one's inner state, one's attitude toward the puzzle. The point of this chapter is that one can intervene with oneself, one can change one's own attitude. Personal success on a series of problems may be desirable, but it is not essential. With little more than a few examples, one can talk oneself into ignoring the threat of failure (the *false* threat of failure— what, after all, are the terrible consequences of failing to solve the cryptarithmetic problem?). One can become more receptive to the challenge, to that quality of attraction produced almost naturally by any puzzle. If one does this, if one deliberately starts to engage problems intimately, to open oneself to the fascination, then the experience of success will start to follow.

"Why should I go to such trouble?" the dismisser might say. "Who cares about cryptarithmetic problems and riddles anyway?" Rather than try to answer these questions for puzzles and riddles, I will use as illustrations an entirely different class of problems, one where the

FIGURE 2.1

D O N A L D

+ G E R A L D

R O B E R T

$D = 5$

A cryptarithmetic problem. Each different letter represents a different digit from 0-9. The same letter always takes the same digit. The result, after replacing the letters with digits, must be a correct addition problem. It is given that $D = 5$.

solutions have material consequences: around-the-house problems—appliance repair and the like.

An appliance (a toaster, a record player, etc.) stops working. What is the meaning of intimate engagement in this context? It means: Study the piece of equipment from all angles. Use your eyes. Turn it over so that you can see all sides. If the appliance is too big, try to get around it and under it. If there are panels that are screwed down remove them. See into it. Use your eyes. Thus you engage the object intimately.

Let me provide a series of examples from my own experience. I'm one of those people who must have had a history of failure at fixing things because I was inhibited about attempting any repairs. I would never remove a screwed-down panel. I always imagined that a spring would pop out along with ten other pieces. I saw myself staring stupidly at a disintegrated clutter. One day, a clothes dryer that we had owned for fifteen years stopped working. In the middle of a cycle it just squealed and stopped. My wife observed that the dryer was old and had gone the way of all machines. I agreed. Come the weekend, we would get a new one. For a few days we had only the defunct dryer in the house. During this time I noticed that the dryer had a panel in the back, bolted down by four screws. Normally, I would never remove such a panel. This time, however, I thought "What harm? Even if I can't put the machine back together, it's dead anyway." So I removed the panel from the dryer (unplugging it first, of course). Nothing happened other than that the back of the machine was revealed. It was stuffed, completely stuffed with lint, a fifteen-year accumulation. I vacuumed it out (noting, incidentally, the remarkable simplicity of the dryer: the large clothing tumbler is driven by a belt that is attached to a motor—that's it) and, behold, it worked perfectly—my first success with intimate engagement.

My second experience happened at the home of another couple. A friend, Sam, and I were visiting them, all of us sitting around a table that wobbled. I commented on its sway. The husband replied in disgust that the table wasn't two years old and this wobbling had started. He was going to get rid of it. I nodded sympathetically, but Sam's response was different. He got under the table and, after a few seconds, invited us to join him. There was nothing mysterious. The legs were attached by screws and the screws had loosened. A few turns of a screwdriver and the table was like new. All one had to do was to get down and look, to engage intimately the problem of the wobbling table.

As chance had it, I subsequently faced a similar problem. My car seat was stuck—I couldn't get it to move forward or back. The usual movement of the lever release at the front of the seat did nothing; the seat wouldn't budge. Previously, I would have muttered a few colorful words and have driven the car to the repair shop. Now, however, I had this new principle. I knelt down and peered under the seat. A wire attached to the release lever had slipped off. I put it back on. Problem solved. Moral: Engage the problem intimately; use your eyes.

Since then I've faced a variety of such problems. I routinely try to take apart a defective appliance. Sometimes I could see the relevant part only by inserting a mirror; sometimes I could only reach a hand underneath and visualize the mechanical linkages by patiently feeling them. It is astonishing how often this intimate engagement, this direct exploration, has revealed a simple structure and has yielded a solution. Frequently, like the dryer, the malfunctioning appliance is simply dirty (e.g., a toaster had a large crumb caught in the pop-up spring); other times an easily replaceable part has obviously broken. It literally pays to engage the problem, to look deeply.

The psychiatrist Scott Peck (1978) has described his own version of intimate engagement, which he refers to as *taking the time*. He first tells how he would never try to repair anything, feeling that he was deficient in mechanical ability. One day he passed a neighbor who was fixing a lawn mower. He paused and remarked to the neighbor that he admired him, that he himself had no ability to repair things. The neighbor replied with one sentence: "That's because you don't take the time." Dr. Peck went his way stunned by this simple truth. There was no defect within himself. He had been making a choice. He had simply refused to engage these problems, to give them the time. As it happened, the opportunity to test this idea soon occurred. In the following passage he describes his first encounter with intimate engagement, with taking the time, when repairing something. As you will see, his description is consistent with all the preceding examples.

> The parking brake was stuck on a patient's car, and she knew that there was something one could do under the dashboard to release it, but she didn't know what. I lay down on the floor below the front seat of her car. Then I took the time to make myself comfortable. Once I was comfortable, I then took the time to look at the situation. I looked for several minutes. At first all I saw was a confusing jumble of wires and tubes and rods, whose meaning I did not know. But gradually, in no hurry, I was able to focus my sight on the brake apparatus and trace its course. And then it became clear to me that there was a little latch preventing the brake from being released. I slowly studied this latch until it became clear to me that if I were to push it upward with the tip of my finger it would move easily and would release the brake. And so I did this. One single motion, one ounce of pressure from a fingertip, and the problem was solved. I was a master mechanic! (Peck, 1978, p. 28)

The concrete problem solving of the sort just described best reveals intimate engagement—it is seen directly in the behavior. But it applies, of course, to all problems. Engaging a problem intimately has two properties. One is motivational: Commit yourself to the problem; give it time and energy; do not be stopped at the outset by your inhibitions. The other entails vision and visual imagery: Use your eyes; visualize the problem task; mentally, as well as physically, "look" at the task from all sides. These dual processes, approaching the problem zestfully and using your eyes, are the essentials of intimate engagement. They apply to all problems.

This principle of intimate engagement raises a question that is relevant to this entire book. In solving a problem, what is the role of background knowledge, of prior learning about the specific topic? Suppose, for example, my car fails to start. Committed to intimate engagement, I open the hood and look into the inner workings. If, however, I know nothing about the battery, solenoids, the motor, and fan belt and their relation to the engine, then I can do little. Not all problems are as simple as seeing and removing dirt. Isn't background knowledge important? The answer is "certainly." In fact, a foundation prescriptive rule, one that is so obvious that no special chapter has been allotted to it, is that if you want to solve problems effectively in a given complex domain (e.g., geometry, car repair, chess) learn as much as you can about that domain. Read in it, explore in it, practice in it.

The need for background knowledge, however, does not argue against intimate engagement; on the contrary, it argues for it. Intimate engagement is a form of exploration. In connection with the example of the dryer, I noted that removing the rear panel led me to see the inner structure of the machine, to see how the tumbler was driven by a motor and a connecting belt. It is true that prior knowledge may be useful (e.g., I was able to recognize a motor). Frequently, however, the sheer engagement of the problem deepens your knowledge of the domain. You not only solve the problem, but you see the inner workings. This, in turn, will make it easier to solve similar problems in the future.

For an illustration of this point, consider Figure 2.2. It shows schematically what I saw when I looked into the dryer. As a result you and I now know a great deal about dryers. Suppose, for example, we push the button to start the dryer and little happens. We hear the motor humming, but the tumbler doesn't turn. We can infer that the belt is probably broken. For another example, suppose that when we push the start button we hear nothing, that is, not even the hum of the motor. We would conclude either that there is a break in the electrical

Start
Button

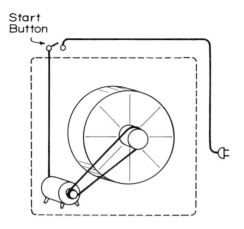

FIGURE 2.2
Portrait of a dryer,
showing the tumbler,
motor, belt, and
switch.

system (it isn't plugged in or the switch is defective) or that the motor needs to be replaced. Thus, troubleshooting is now easy because of previous exploration, because of the intimate engagement of an earlier problem.

We may conclude, then, that although background knowledge (here, knowledge about dryers) is important, intimate engagement is a powerful procedure for gaining that knowledge. This conclusion is reinforced by a slightly more complex version of intimate engagement. Suppose a piece of equipment is not working and you now, having learned this principle, look inside, study it, and see nothing that is obviously wrong. What can you do next? If you have a duplicate that is working, study that duplicate. Look inside of it. See how the parts are related and move in the intact system; then return to the defective appliance. Now you may notice that a spring in the good one is missing in the other, or that a screw has fallen out, or that something else didn't match.

Recently I was with a friend when he discovered that he had a problem that I had faced earlier—his car seat wouldn't slide back on the track; it was stuck. I offered to help. Of course, I got down and peered underneath the seat. Nevertheless, I couldn't see anything that might be wrong. Now what could be done? Well, the car was a two-seater and the seat on the passenger side was working. I went around to the other side, got down by the passenger seat and studied it. I saw how it operated, what the linkages were as I moved the release lever and pushed the seat back and forth. When I went back to look at the underside of the defective seat it was now obvious that a spring was missing. It had fallen off and was lying half-hidden by the seat track. I hooked it into the location that I remembered from the other seat; the problem was instantly solved. Thus, a corollary to "use your eyes" is "if necessary, study a working model."

You might complain that this last rule is too limiting. "O.K.," you might argue, "a car happens to have two similar seats. But who has two dryers or two toasters? How can we study a working model?" Here we extend the activity of intimate engagement still further, but in a plausible direction. A neighbor of mine tells this story. He had a lawn mower that he had trouble starting. Studying it closely didn't reveal the defect. A duplicate model was not available. He simply went to the library and took out a book on the repair of lawn mowers. The book showed pictures of a working model, revealing the inner connections necessary for smooth starting. He was now able, book in hand, to look at his mower, compare the two, and to solve the problem. The moral is, again, that intimate engagement, especially of this richer sort, leads to knowledge. It is not only a way to solve your problem, it is an effective form of exploration.

3

USE YOUR EYES, EXTERNALIZE:

The Intimate
Engagement
of Mathematical
and Logical Puzzles

When I was a college freshman, taking my first calculus course, the professor announced: "Don't get in the habit of learning mathematics from my lectures. The way to learn math is by yourself, with a book, a pad, and a pencil."

The point of this statement seems clear enough. *You should not rely on others to teach you. Rather, you should get into the habit of learning on your own. That way you can continue to learn and grow when you have left college, when teachers are not so handy. All you would need is a book.* That certainly seems like a reasonable interpretation. Why, however, did he add that you needed a pad and a pencil? That you need a book to learn on your own is self-evident, but why the other materials?

The answer to that question has emerged from psychological research in the last twenty-five years. We need these supplementary aids because the conscious mind is remarkably limited in the amount of activity it can perform. The conscious mind engages in three important processes: (1) It receives external information via the senses and interprets this information, as when you look at a scene or when you hear someone speaking. Right now your conscious mind is taking in and trying to interpret the words on this page. (2) It "displays" the information when you are remembering something, whether it is an incident from several years ago, the face of a friend, a song, or a phone number that you read 10 seconds ago. (3) It manipulates information that is being remembered, as when you imagine things (example: picture in your head, that is, remember, the American flag; now imagine it, not with red-and-white stripes, but with green-and-white stripes).

The first fact of our limitations is that we cannot do all three things at once—at least not well. If, as you are reading, you start thinking about last night's date, you will find that, although your eyes have moved over the page, you cannot remember a thing that you have read. If you are trying to hold a phone number in your mind long enough to get to the telephone, an interruption (your kid brother stops you and asks for a quarter) will frequently cause it to be forgotten.

The eminent psychologist George Miller first noted this odd limitation of human consciousness about thirty years ago (Miller, 1956). He proposed that we can deal with only about six or seven items of information. With more than that, the mind becomes overloaded, and we start to lose some of the information. That is why a momentarily remembered phone number is so vulnerable to forgetting. It contains seven digits. If while rehearsing it, you are distracted by your kid brother, that demand on your conscious attention overloads consciousness. Some of the digits get lost.

A famous experiment, first performed by Collin Cherry (1953), has a person who is wearing earphones hear a different message come into each ear. Thus, a voice reading from a history book may be heard in the right ear and, simultaneously, a voice reading from a novel may be heard in the left ear. The listener is given a special task called "shadowing," that is, is asked to repeat word-for-word what is heard in the right ear. Suppose this shadowing is carried on for 5 minutes. Following this the person is asked questions about what was heard in both the right and the left ear. The startling result is that the person can tell you virtually nothing about what was presented to the left (the nonshadowed) ear. Not only is the content of the passage lost but if, for about 2 minutes in the middle of right-ear shadowing, the language in the left ear changes from English to Russian, the person fails to notice that. It is as though the right-ear shadowing used up all the capacity of the conscious mind. The information from the left ear could not get in.

This fact, that the conscious mind is severely restricted in how much it can do, affects problem solving, of course. This limitation may be illustrated with an obvious example. Consider these two numbers: 483 and 627. Read them a few times. Make sure you know them so that you can say them without looking. Now, look away from the book and multiply them in your head.

*   *   *   *   *   *   *   *   *

If you are like most people you can picture placing one number above the other, ready for multiplication. However, when you try to carry out in imagination the step-by-step multiplication procedures you find that it is next to impossible. Why is that? You certainly know how to multiply. The reason should by now be clear. The six digits in those two numbers are about the limit of what the conscious mind can deal with. If, in addition to remembering those two numbers, you now try to manipulate the information, to imagine multiplying and adding, the system becomes overloaded. You fail to carry out even a well-known routine.

How, then, do we obtain the product of those two numbers? Obviously, we look for a pad and a pencil. These tools are supplements to the conscious mind. It no longer has to do everything. The pad and pencil permit us to "externalize" the two numbers. Once they are written down, the conscious mind doesn't have to keep remembering them. It can now expend its resources on the procedures of multiplication. In general, when you use a pad and a pencil, this precious but limited resource that we call consciousness doesn't have to be used up just on remembering things.

Here are a couple of additional examples. First, try to solve each problem in your head. Then take out a pencil and paper and work the problem that way. See for yourself the difference that "externalizing" makes.

A rectangular board is sawed into two pieces by a straight cut across its width. The larger piece is twice the length of the smaller piece. This smaller piece is cut again into two parts, one three times the length of the other. You now have three pieces of board. The smallest piece is a 7-inch square. What was the original area of the surface of the board?

*   *   *   *   *   *   *   *   *

Here is a problem for you geometry buffs. Again, first read the problem so that you understand it and, without drawing the figure on paper, try to solve it in your head. Then draw the figure, making appropriate marks as needed. See how much easier it is to solve.

Starting with the upper left-hand corner and going clockwise, the corners of a square are labeled *A, B, C,* and *D,* respectively. From the midpoint of the left-hand vertical line (line *AD*), a straight line is drawn to vertex *C.* The diagonal *BD* is also drawn in. These two lines intersect in some point that we will call *E.* What is the ratio of length *DE* to length *EB*?

The answers to these two problems are given in Appendix A.

*   *   *   *   *   *   *   *   *

We said that externalizing the information relieves the conscious mind from having actively to display the information. The mind is then free for the problem-solving activity itself. However, externalizing does a bit more than that. It also produces a tight interaction between the eyes, the hand, and the mind. It helps us, in short, to engage the problem more intimately.

Now that you are persuaded of the value of using a pad and pencil in studying math (You probably knew it all along. Let's just say we analyzed why it is valuable), you might think there is nothing left to say. "O.K.," you reply, "from now on when I study math I'll keep a pad and pencil handy." That's that. Externalizing, however, has another virtue. There are standard ways of ordering the information on paper for certain classes of problems. These methods are not always obvious, and so I want to present a few of them here.

MATRIX PROBLEMS

In some logic problems, it is helpful to put the information into a table, or *matrix.* I will illustrate this method first and will then present a couple of problems that you can try on your own.

Tom, Dick, Harry, and Al are married to May, Jane, Sue, and Bea, though not necessarily in that order. Jane, who is Dick's sister, has five children. Tom and his wife want to wait a few more years before starting a family. Tom has never introduced his wife to Sue, who is carrying on an extramarital affair with Dick. (May is considering telling Dick's wife about it.) Dick and Harry, by the way, are twin brothers. Who is married to whom?

Again, you might first try to solve this problem in your head. After that, try it again using a paper and pencil. You may now notice a new problem. How should you organize the information on paper? Just writing the relations into a list as you think of them may be helpful, but it is not the most effective method. There is a way to be systematic about the information you put on paper so as to make the relationships more obvious. The limitation of a list is that it goes in only one dimension, that is, from the top down. This problem, however, has two categories, a set of men and a set of women. We would like to organize the information to reflect that. We would like, that is, a two-dimensional way of recording the information. Figure 3.1 shows the outlines of a matrix that does just that. Each row shows for each man four "cells" corresponding to the four possible wives. Similarly, each column shows for each woman four possible-husband cells. We can now proceed to fill in the information that is given. We are told, by implication, that Jane is not married to Dick, so we can put an X in the corresponding cell (that is, at the intersection of the Dick row and the Jane column). For the same reason, Jane is not married to Harry, and, because she has children and Tom does not, is not married to Tom. Putting X's into those two corresponding cells, we see that there is only one remaining possibility for Jane. She must be married to Al. Let us indicate that by putting a circle into that cell. We may also note the following: X's may be put into the other three cells in Al's row since he is married to Jane and not those other three ladies. At this point the matrix has the

FIGURE 3.1
A matrix arrangement of the husbands and wives.

appearance shown in Figure 3.2. Continue filling it in until you have the complete solution. The rest of the answer is in Appendix A.

Here is a similar problem for you to practice on.

Roger, Harry, George, and Mark work in the city as singer, stockbroker, salesman, and cook (but not necessarily in that order). Harry car pools with the salesman and the singer. Mark plays bridge with the salesman and the cook. The cook drives to work alone. Roger envies the salesman. Which man has which career?

The next problem is somewhat different in that it involves numbers. You will again find that a matrix is useful. In addition, however, numbers have arithmetical properties that become part of the solution.

Three boys, Joey, Jimmy, and Pete, have between them nine quarters and a total of $2.55 in quarters and nickels. Joey has three nickels, and Jimmy has the same number of quarters. Jimmy has one coin more than Joey, who has four coins. How many nickels each do Jimmy and Pete have?

The matrix for each of these last two problems is in Appendix A.

Here is an interesting problem that the problem-solving theorist John Hayes claims to have solved by use of a matrix. First, try solving it your own way, then read on.

An anthropologist, back from a field trip, was invited to a party with her husband. Always the scientist, she decided to observe and to make measurements of the curious American ritual of handshaking. Four other married couples attended the party. Whenever two people shook hands, she recorded that each of the two people shook hands one time. In that way, for all of them (including herself and her husband), she obtained the total number of times that each person shook hands. First, she noted two obvious facts. One didn't shake hands with one's own spouse, and one didn't shake the same person's hand twice. Then she

	May	Jane	Sue	Bea
Tom		X		
Dick		X		
Harry		X		
Al	X	O	X	X

FIGURE 3.2
The husbands-wives
matrix partially filled in.

looked at her list and observed an odd fact. If she didn't count herself, the other nine people all shook hands a different number of times. That is, one person didn't shake any hands, one shook only once, up to one shaking the hands of all eight of the others.

Question: How many times did her husband shake hands?

Isn't this an elegant problem? You would swear at first that you have not been given enough information to solve it. A biochemist that I know, when he heard this problem, exclaimed "Sure! You might as well ask what was the color of his tie."

Since this problem is a bit difficult, let me include a hint. Can the anthropologist's husband be the one who shook hands eight times, that is, with all the other couples? No, because then each of those eight people would have shaken hands with at least one person (the anthropologist's husband), and it is given that one of the nine people shook hands with no one. Try to solve this problem now; then read on to see Hayes's approach.

*   *   *   *   *   *   *   *   *

Hayes laid out a matrix similar to the one in Figure 3.3, where the husbands and wives, *H* and *W*, are numbered as couples. Here, X's are placed in the cells where people definitely did not shake hands with

FIGURE 3.3   A matrix for the anthropologist problem showing the tentative assumption that H_1 shook hands with all the other couples.

each other. Assume for the moment that couple 5 is the anthropologist and her husband. For want of anything better to do, Hayes assumed that husband 1, H_1, was the person who shook hands with everyone else, and filled in checkmarks in the H_1 row for everyone (excluding, of course, H_1 and his wife). Note that each of the other eight people shook hands at least once, that is, with H_1. This beginning, says Hayes, "yielded the first important insight into the problem. Since everyone but H_1's wife shook hands at least once, she is the only person who could have shaken hands zero times" (Hayes, 1981, p. 65 ff.).

Incidentally, note the value here of externalizing. Relieving the mind of having to organize all the information makes it easier to have insights.

X's may now be placed in the row and column for W_1. Try making H_2 be the person who shook hands seven times, and continue on. See if you cannot solve the problem using the matrix. The complete analysis and the answer is given in Appendix A.

FUNCTION GENERATING PROBLEMS

Another type of problem that lends itself to systematic externalization of information involves determining a general function for a large number of events. The plan is to look at the results for small numbers of corresponding events and to see if a pattern doesn't emerge. A couple of simple examples will make this clear.

> A gambler bets 3 dollars on the first spin of a roulette wheel. Each time he loses he doubles his bet. He has lost n times in a row. How do we express $A_{n + 1}$, the amount of his bet for the next (the $n + 1$) spin?

This problem is simple enough that you can probably do it in your head, but we can conveniently use it to illustrate the method. Make a table, with two columns, the left one labeled "Number of spins, n" and the right column labeled "Amount bet, A." Begin, in the first row, with the smallest possible n. In this case, let n be 1, the first spin, for which it is given that he bet 3 dollars. For the next spin, for $n = 2$, he will bet $3 * 2 = 6$ dollars. For the third spin he will bet $(3 * 2) * 2 = 12$ dollars, and so on. Figure 3.4 shows the table carried out for five spins. We study the table to see the pattern that emerges. We see that the amount bet, A, is always 3 multiplied by 2 with some exponent. Furthermore, for each spin that exponent is increased by one, and is always one less than the number of the spin. This leads to the plausible generalization that the amount of money bet on the nth spin, A_n, is given by

NUMBER OF SPINS, n	AMOUNT BET, A
1	3
2	$3 * 2 = 6$
3	$3 * 2^2 = 12$
4	$3 * 2^3 = 24$
5	$3 * 2^4 = 48$

FIGURE 3.4   Generation of the pattern $A_{n+1} = 3 * 2^n$.

$$A_n = 3 * 2^{n-1}$$

On the next spin, the amount, A_{n+1}, will be

$$A_{n+1} = 3 * 2^n$$

If the poor fellow loses ten times in a row, on the next spin he will bet $3 * 2^{10} = 3 * 1,024$ or 3,072 dollars.

Here is another problem that benefits from this mode of externalizing the information.

New York City decides to hold a handball tournament to determine the city handball champion. The contest will follow "knockout" rules: In the first round each contestant will be randomly paired with another; each pair plays one game; the loser is permanently out of the contest. (If an odd number of players entered the contest, then, at the first round, one person "draws a bye," that is, doesn't play until the second round.) At the second round, the winners, and the person who had drawn a bye, are randomly paired. The process repeats for as many rounds as needed until only one player, the city champion, remains.

Suppose n people sign up for the tournament. How many games must be played to determine the champion? (A game, remember, is defined as two people playing until one of them wins.)

See if you can't work out the answer using a table similar to the one in the preceding problem. Suppose two people sign up (that is, $n = 2$). How many games must be played? Continue the investigation for $n = 3, 4, 5$, and so on.

$$*\quad*\quad*\quad*\quad*\quad*\quad*\quad*\quad*$$

The pattern suggests that with n contestants then $n - 1$ games must be played. Look back over the table you have generated. Can you see why there *must* be exactly one game less than the number of players? If it does not jump out at you now, see Appendix A.

For another example, consider this next problem.

> You are going to a swanky gambling casino. Entrance to the casino is itself based upon a gamble as follows: At the entranceway is a machine that, when you put in 1 dollar, randomly produces a card in one of ten different colors. You need five matching cards (five red, or five white, and so on) to enter the casino. How much must you be prepared to spend to enter? To put this question another way, what is the maximum, *M*, you may be required to spend? In general, suppose there are *n* different colors and you must obtain *k* matching cards. How much must you be prepared to spend?

This time we have two variables, the number of colors, n, and the number of required matching cards, k. Let us first begin with small values of n and increase it (keeping k small and constant. Begin by assuming that we need only two matching cards, that is, take $k = 2$. After seeing the role that n plays, we will systematically increase k). Figure 3.5 shows the table for increasing values of n.

NUMBER OF DIFFERENT COLORS, *n*	MAXIMUM NUMBER OF DOLLARS, *M*
2	3
3	4
4	5

FIGURE 3.5 The maximum number of dollars that may be spent as the number of colors increases. Here, two matching cards are required (i.e., *k* = 2).

When there are just two colors ($n = 2$) and we are required to get a matching pair, then we must be prepared to spend 3 dollars: The first two cards may be different; the third card *must* match one of them. By similar reasoning, if there are three colors, then the first three cards may all be different. The fourth must produce a match. In general, M, the maximum number of cards needed to get two the same, is one more than the number of different colors used. (If there are n colors, the first n cards may all be different; the $n + 1$st card *must* produce a match.) Thus, when $k = 2$,

$$M = n + 1$$

Suppose, now, that n is large. What happens as k becomes larger than 2? Suppose we need three matching cards, or four, or five. Now how do we express M? Again let us prepare a table (see Figure 3.6). For $k = 2$ we have seen that we need $n + 1$ cards. Suppose $k = 3$. Well, we can get two of each of the n colors and still not have the needed three-card match. In such a case, however, one more card would do it. In other words, to get a three-card match, we may have to buy $2 * n + 1$ cards. By similar reasoning, for four matching cards, we may need $3 * n + 1$. This and the value for five are shown in the table. What pattern do we see? In general, what is M? We see in the table that the coefficient of n increases by one each time and is always one less than k. In short,

$$M = (k - 1) * n + 1$$

If, as we said at the outset, the machine has ten colors and requires five matches, you may have to spend as much as 41 dollars to enter.

NUMBER OF MATCHING CARDS, k	MAXIMUM NUMBER OF DOLLARS, M
2	$n + 1$
3	$2 * n + 1$
4	$3 * n + 1$
5	$4 * n + 1$

FIGURE 3.6   **The maximum number of dollars that may be spent as the number of matching cards, k, increases. It is assumed that the number of colors, n, is fixed.**

INTIMATE ENGAGEMENT

4

USE YOUR EYES, VISUALIZE:

The Problem of Comprehension

For a different application of intimate engagement I want to consider the problem of comprehension, the problem of trying to understand written or spoken material—a piece, say, of expository prose.

Ernest Hemingway, in *For Whom the Bell Tolls,* provides us with a pertinent definition of good writing. The American soldier in Spain, Robert Jordan, has just listened to a Spanish peasant, Pilar, tell how the communists took over her village. He reflects on her tale:

"Pilar had made him see it in that town. If that woman could only write."

He later reflects again how she had made him "see" the events.

Thus, good writing makes the reader see the story; it lights up images in the reader's mind. However, communication between a writer and reader is not a one-way process; it does not depend only upon vivid prose. The writer must be effective, but the reader must do his or her share. The reader must be prepared to imagine the information, to make his or her mind light up. Not every writer is a virtuoso. Important information may have to be communicated by someone less skillful than Hemingway. In such a case the reader must make an effort to "penetrate" the information, must try to visualize what is being described, to "see" the interrelationship of facts presented. This is intimate engagement of verbal material.

To show the role that the reader plays in comprehension, I'll use an extreme example. A woman I know wanted to work as a volunteer for a first-aid organization. To do so she first had to pass a test based entirely (she said) upon a book provided by the organization. The book described various injuries and the corresponding treatment. For example, for treatment of a broken arm, it said:

A. Broken limbs
    1. Lower arm: For a lower arm fracture the following two steps are to be taken:
        a. Splint with board or folded newspapers
        b. Secure arm with sling

One day she called me over and asked me to quiz her on her knowledge of the material. I opened the book to, as it chanced, the section on broken limbs and asked: "What two steps must be taken if someone has broken the lower part of his arm?" She said: "They won't ask such questions. You have to say 'Broken limbs,' 'lower arm.' " I dutifully replied, "O.K. 'Broken limbs,' 'lower arm.' " To which she recited word for word: "For a lower arm fracture, . . ." I then did that at another place and was given a similar rote recall. She occasionally blocked in the middle of an answer and had to start over, but, on the whole, was satisfied with her performance. I then asked, "Suppose you see an accident where someone complains that his arms feel broken, what will you do?" She said, "They won't ask that. You just have to know what is in this book."

You will not be surprised to learn that she failed the test. The point, of course, is that she failed to engage the material. Instead of visualizing the person, the broken arm, the bandages, the splints, she saw only the words for these things. She didn't play her part as the receiver of the information; she didn't let her mind light up.

This is an extreme example, one that, of course, does not apply to you or to me, but it highlights by contrast what needs to be done.

Research during the last fifteen years has solidly buttressed this thesis, that visualizing is *the* powerful way to comprehend written material. The following examples, adapted from Bransford and Johnson (1972), will permit you to experience this for yourself. Read the following passage with the idea that you will be taking an examination on this material tomorrow.

A newspaper is better than a magazine. A seashore is a better place than the street. At first it is better to run than to walk. You may have to try several times. It takes some skill but it's easy to learn. Even young children can have fun.

Once successful, complications are minimal. Birds seldom get too close. Too many people doing the same thing, however, can cause problems. One needs lots of room. Beware of rain; it ruins everything. If there are no complications, it can be very peaceful. A rock will serve as an anchor. If things break loose from it, however, you will not get a second chance.

Every sentence seems to make sense, but if you are like most people you have the uneasy sense that you really didn't understand the passage. Go back and reread it now with the information that the passage deals with *flying kites*.

* * * * * * * * *

Do you see the difference in your comprehension this second time? You could "see" (visualize) everything that is referred to. It is almost as though this visualizing is virtually synonymous with understanding.

Here is another opportunity to contrast reading without and with visualizing. Read the next passage also with the thought that you will later be tested on the information.

The procedure is actually quite simple. First, you arrange things into different groups. Of course, one pile may be sufficient depending on how much there is to do. If you have to go somewhere else due to lack of facilities, that is the next step; otherwise, you are pretty well set. It is important not to overdo things. That is, it is better to do too few things at once than too many.

After the procedure is completed, one arranges the materials into different groups again. Then they can be put into their appropriate places. Eventually they will be used once more and the whole cycle will then have to be repeated. However, that is part of life.

As before, I am going to give the title of this passage and to ask you to read it again. Let me urge you to pay some attention to how different your experience is this second time, to how much more visual it is. The passage is about *washing clothes*. Reread it now.

*   *   *   *   *   *   *   *   *

Once you key into the topic of the passage, and are able to visualize the information, it becomes much more a part of you. Bransford and Johnson had two groups of college students study these passages. One group was given the topic information (e.g., that the first passage was about flying kites) before reading the passage; the other group was given the topic only after the reading. On a later test of the information, the first group scored twice as high as the second. Visualizing is clearly an important process for comprehending. Better comprehension, in turn, produces better remembering.

In our discussion of comprehension thus far, we have used "seeing" to mean imagining, mentally picturing a scene. When we discuss visualizing and remembering in the next chapter, we will see further evidence that this mental picturing is a powerful technique. When the prose passage involves numbers, however, "seeing" can mean something deeper. It refers to apprehending or grasping the logic, the connections among the numbers. One doesn't necessarily visualize a scene; one, rather, strives for a sense of how the numbers are related. When you have "seen" in this sense, two effects typically appear. You know, by inference, information not directly given in the passage. Also, the numbers "make sense," that is, you understand why the author used those numbers and not some others.

Let us begin with an elementary example to remind you how relationships among numbers permit inferences. Consider the following passage, which might appear in a children's story.

As Jack walked to town he met three beggars. He gave them each 4 dollars. That left only 2 dollars for himself, but he didn't care. He felt happy.

Notice that if we think about it, we can infer that Jack started with 14 dollars. Furthermore, they were probably all singles.

Here is a slightly more difficult version.

Jack stuffed the 16 dollar bills into his wallet and decided to go to town to buy a toy. He left his house and walked a half-mile when he met a beggar. The man seemed so poor that Jack gave him half the money in his wallet. About every half-mile he was approached by another beggar, each more wretched than the last. He met the third one just at the outskirts of town. Jack gave to each one half the money in his wallet. As he left the third beggar and entered the town he saw that he had only 2 dollars left but he didn't care. He felt happy.

1. Does that final figure of 2 dollars make sense to you? Do you see how it follows from the other numerical details given in the story?
2. Did Jack have any money in his wallet before he put in the 16 dollars? (For example, could he already have had 8 dollars?)
3. Approximately how far is Jack's house from the edge of town?

*   *   *   *   *   *   *   *   *

Note the word "see" in the first set of questions. That usage does not seem to imply "visualize" in the sense of vividly imagining a scene. Rather, it refers to a process that is more abstract; it refers to developing an awareness of the relationships among the numbers. Thus, we "see" that when we start with 16 and halve it three times, we end up with 2.

The preceding examples were introductory and elementary. The next examples are more realistic and challenging. They are modeled on descriptions of psychology experiments that may be found routinely in the research literature. Try to read each passage carefully enough that you can answer the questions at the end without having to reread. Since the material is numerical and a bit technical, you may want to follow the prescription of the last chapter and *externalize;* that is, you would do well to use a pad and pencil.

Fifteen subjects (college freshmen) were used in this experiment. Each subject heard a list of sentences of the noun-verb-noun form (e.g., The girl sees the dog). These sentences were either positive (The motorcycle scratched the car) or negative (The truck is not carrying the bicycle), and this variable was combined with the variable of verb tense. That is, for each of the two kinds of sentences, the verb could be future, present, or past tense. Five sentences of each of the six types were constructed.

All the sentences were read to the subject one time. Following this reading of the list of sentences, a recall test was presented. The first noun in the sentence (e.g., The motorcycle) was stated, and the subject had to write the entire sentence. A response was scored correct only if both the verb and second noun were correctly given. The 450 responses were evaluated in this way.

1. Why does the author say that there were six types of sentences? What were these six types?
2. How many different sentences were constructed? Why were there 450 responses?

*   *   *   *   *   *   *   *   *

Here is another example:

Eighty students served in this experiment on problem solving. Each student received one of four similar problems (referred to as problems A, B, C, and D). Since we were interested in the effects of distraction, half the students worked on their problem with music playing; half worked in silence. The ten students in each condition consisted of one eight-year-old, four ten-year-olds, and five twelve-year-old children.

1. How many conditions were there? What were they?
2. Why does the author refer to ten students?
3. How many eight-year-olds served in this experiment?

*   *   *   *   *   *   *   *   *

And another:

Thirty-six students (eighteen males and eighteen females) served in an experiment on problem solving. Each of these students rceived three problems, A, B, and C. Since each subject was receiving all three problems, the sequence of problem presentation was varied. All possible variations (BCA, CAB, etc.) were used. Three males and three females were assigned to each of the six different sequences.

1. Why were there six different sequences? Could there have been more than this number? What were these six sequences?
2. Did the number of students used, thirty six, strike you as unusual? Why did the experimenter use such a number instead of a nice, round number like thirty or forty? What other numbers might the experimenter have used?

In reading each passage, most of you, I suspect, followed the description and felt that you understood the material. Nevertheless, you were surprised by the questions. If you had asked yourself these questions as you were reading, then you had intimately engaged the material; if not then your reading was too superficial, not penetrating. Go back now and reread the passages, this time with the questions in mind. Notice how it will improve your ability to visualize the entire experiment.

A subtle difficulty arises in considering intimate engagement applied to language (text or lecture). Many of you feel fooled by the preceding passages. You felt that you understood them as you were reading. How could you know that you were not engaging the material sufficiently closely? The answer to this requires two qualities:

First, you must become more sensitive to your own confusion. As you are reading and trying to comprehend a passage, an inner bell should ring whenever something puzzling occurs. Suppose an author writes, "It is obvious, therefore, that each subject will require six problems." Is it obvious to you? Or are you puzzled by that number? Become sensitive to your own state of confusion—have that bell go off.

Second, do not permit yourself to be confused. Work out the relationships. Use a pad and pencil, if necessary. At a lecture raise your hand: "It is not obvious to me, professor. Would you please explain it? Would you please give an example?"[1] Do not tolerate confusion. Heed the bell! If you're studying for a course and, in spite of your best efforts, something in the book just doesn't make sense, ask your classmates, or your teacher, or check in the library for easier explanatory material. Push to penetrate until you can see what is being discussed. That's intimate engagement.

[1] I have a favorite "It-is-obvious" anecdote (apocryphal) that I can't resist passing along here. A math professor was explaining a complex proof, writing it step by step on the blackboard. He said, "Now it is obvious that steps 10 and 11 lead to the following equation," and he wrote that equation on the board. One student raised his hand and said, "Sir, it's not obvious to me that that equation follows from 10 and 11. Would you please explain it?" The professor turned to the blackboard and studied it intently. After a full 20 minutes he turned back to the class and announced, "Yes, it is obvious!"

Section II
(continued)

INTIMATE ENGAGEMENT

5

USE YOUR EYES, VISUALIZE:

Committing Information to Memory

In the previous chapter we saw that visualizing is not only important for comprehension, but that this mental seeing leads to better remembering. Several lines of research provide evidence for this principle, that when your problem is to remember new information, visualizing helps. Perhaps the most direct application of the power of picturing images while reading comes from Levin and Pressley with children and from Anderson with adults. Levin (1973) instructed a group of fourth-grade children to visualize as they read. Each child was simply told "to think of a picture in his mind of each sentence's contents as he read the passage." The children then read a twelve-sentence story. A second group received identical treatment except that the special instruction to picture the contents was omitted. On a subsequent test, the instructed group recalled 20 percent more than did uninstructed children. Pressley (1976) demonstrated a similar effect with third-grade children.

It is not only young children who benefit from instructions to visualize as they read. Anderson and Hidde (1971) had two groups of college students read a list of thirty sentences, each of the form: The/*noun*/*verb*/the/*noun* (e.g., The girl caught the robin). One group was instructed to form an image as they read each sentence; the other group was instructed, instead, to read each sentence three times. A recall test followed the reading of the sentence list. For each of the sentences, the first noun (e.g., "The girl") was given, and the student had to complete the sentence. The imagery group recalled three times as many sentences as the repetition group. Anderson (Anderson and Kulhavy, 1972) followed up this demonstration with a more natural task. He tested college students on their reading of a 2,000-word passage. Students who reported visualizing the information remembered sustantially more than did students who failed to visualize.

Thus, from both the work on comprehension and on remembering, the lesson is clear. When your problem is to remember what you read, visualizing as you read is an important strategy. Start practicing it now, if you do not already do so. At first you will be self-conscious about the activity. You will have the sense that you are actively engaging the material that you are reading. Later, visualizing will become a habit, and you will simply be a better reader.

This strategy that we have just discussed, of visualizing to aid remembering, is "natural" in the sense that it employs an available cognitive process (although, as we have just seen, it is a process that some people neglect or have never learned to use). The remaining applications of visualizing to aid remembering are more artificial. They are *mnemonic devices,* memory tricks that are employed to produce better recall of particular information. Before we begin our discussion of these, it is important that you look at Figure 5.1. Read and follow the directions given in that figure. After you have completed the task, return to your reading.

Directions

First: Take a piece of paper and cover the list of ten words below. [Do that now.]
Second: Uncover the words one at a time. Study each word by saying it over and over to yourself for about 5 seconds, then go on to the next word and do the same thing. Continue in this way until you come to the end of the list. When you have gone through the list *one time* do not look back at it but return to your reading.

1. Baseball
2. Record
3. Officer
4. Spoon
5. Carpet
6. Chair
7. Palace
8. Gloves
9. Radio
10. Flower

FIGURE 5.1   **A word-learning problem. Begin by reading the directions at the top.**

*   *   *   *   *   *   *   *   *

One of the first mnemonic devices to make its appearance in the modern psychological literature employs a nursery rhyme. Its use as a memory aid was first introduced by Miller, Galanter, and Pribram (1960) with a charming anecdote. I have reprinted it here in its entirety. It describes the rhyme and illustrates one way in which it might be used to help us remember. (*Note:* In this excerpt, Miller et al. use the term "Plan," which is roughly equivalent to the term "strategy." As we do here, these authors assume that trying to remember new information is a problem to be solved.)

One evening we were entertaining a visiting colleague, a social psychologist of broad interests, and our discussion turned to Plans. "But exactly what is a Plan?" he asked. "How can you say that *memorizing* depends on Plans?"

"We'll show you," we replied. "Here is a Plan that you can use for memorizing. Remember first that:

one is a bun,
two is a shoe,
three is a tree,

four is a door,
five is a hive,
six are sticks,
seven is heaven,
eight is a gate,
nine is a line, and
ten is a hen."

"You know, even though it is only ten-thirty here, my watch says one-thirty. I'm really tired, and I'm sure I'll ruin your experiment."

"Don't worry, we have no real stake in it." We tightened our grip on his lapel. "Just relax and remember the rhyme. Now you have part of the Plan. The second part works like this: when we tell you a word, you must form a ludicrous or bizarre association with the first word in your list, and so on with the ten words we recite to you."[2]

"Really, you know, it'll never work. I'm awfully tired," he replied.

"Have no fear," we answered, "just remember the rhyme and then form the association. Here are the words:

1. ashtray,
2. firewood,
3. picture,
4. cigarette,
5. table,
6. matchbook,
7. glass,
8. lamp,
9. shoe,
10. phonograph."

The words were read one at a time, and after reading the word, we waited until he announced that he had the association. It took about 5 seconds on the average to form the connection. After the seventh word he said that he was sure the first six were already forgotten. But we persevered.

After one trial through the list, we waited a minute or two so that he could collect himself and ask any questions that came to mind. Then we said, "What is number eight?"

He stared blankly, and then a smile crossed his face, "I'll be damned," he said. "It's 'lamp.' "

"And what number is cigarette?"

He laughed outright now, and then gave the correct answer.

"And there is no strain," he said, "absolutely no sweat."

[2]Let me spell this out. The visitor is being asked to take each successive word and to put it into an image (Miller et al. use the old-fashioned term, association) with each successive noun in the rhyme. Thus, the first word, *ashtray*, is to be put into a bizarre image with the noun, *bun* (e.g., the visitor might picture an ashtray "sandwich," an ashtray between two halves of a bun). This instruction was made explicit in subsequent formal research.

We proceeded to demonstrate that he could in fact name every word correctly.*

To appreciate the extent of the visitor's accomplishment, take the following test of your memory of the words in Figure 5.1. (Do *not* look back at Figure 5.1 at this time.)

What was the eighth word?
What number in the list was the word "carpet"?
Take a pencil and paper and write, in the sequence that they were presented, all the words that you can recall.

Now look at Figure 5.1. How many did you get right?

The chief difference between you and the visitor in the anecdote is that you used the standard rote-rehearsal method for learning the list. The visitor *visualized* each item in a bizarre image. His performance was a hint of the power of visualizing in remembering. This hint was subsequently incorporated into a formal experiment by Bugelski, Kidd, and Segmer (1968). They had two groups of college students learn lists of words. Both groups first learned the one-is-a-bun jingle and then learned the word list. One group was instructed to learn the list using the visualizing method described by Miller et al. The second group used only the rote-rehearsal method. The visualizing people remembered 40 percent more words than did those using rote-rehearsal. We see again that "picturing means remembering." It enhances learning and retention.

Two sets of applications have followed from this work. The first, related to counting, is based on informal data derived from my own experience. The other application is related to learning vocabulary words in a foreign language. Here the method has been illustrated and verified in laboratory research.

The first example, in which the one-is-a-bun ditty is used in counting, came from a clinical psychologist friend of mine. He regularly taught deep-relaxation methods to clients suffering from psychological stress. One of the methods entailed sitting or lying quietly and breathing deeply. The client was to do this until he had taken twenty breaths. (This focus on breathing while trying to relax was to block out any disturbing thoughts about one's job or family, etc.) He said that frequently clients would complain that they "lost count." At some point in the series, they would stop and say that they didn't know how many breaths they had already taken. His solution to this was to

---

*Miller, George A., Galanter, Eugene, & Pribram, Karl H. (1960). *Plans and the structure of behavior* (pp. 134–136). New York: Henry Holt.

train them to use the one-is-a-bun rhyme. His instructions were: Instead of just saying "one" to yourself, picture a bun; when you say "two," picture a shoe; and so forth; when you come to eleven start over. This problem, he said, was solved. His clients never again had trouble keeping count.

As chance had it, another counting problem came to my attention a few weeks later. A colleague and I were discussing memory problems in everyday life. She mentioned a particular problem that she had been having while swimming. She swam every day for several laps but found that she frequently lost count of the laps. Her explanation was that she was also monitoring her stroke, checking that it was following a 1-2-3-4 rhythm. The number sequence of her stroke, she felt, interfered with the numbering of the laps, and so she lost count.

Well, dear reader, do you have the solution for her problem? I suggested that instead of counting the laps with numbers, she use the one-is-a-bun rhyme (with which she was already familiar). Picture a bun on the first lap, a shoe on the second, and so on. She tried and reported back that it worked like a charm. It was easy to do and the problem was eliminated.

The second application of visualizing to solve a remembering problem is, as I mentioned, to the learning of vocabulary words in a foreign language. This method entails a critical change in the one-is-a-bun technique. In fact, the rhyme is not used. Remembering by using the rhyme, as in the anecdote quoted, is referred to as the *pegword method*. The word "bun," for example, is a "peg" to which the word to be remembered is attached with imagery. In vocabulary learning you use the "keyword" method. Here, instead of using the rhyme words as the pegs, new pegwords are continually created. After that, the methods are the same. For example, suppose your homework assignment consists of learning a long list of French-English vocabulary pairs. Let us say that the first pair is *le chien* = the dog. Using the keyword method, you first think of an English word that sounds like the French word (here, for example, you might use "chin" as similar to *chien*). Next, you put the keyword, chin, into a bizarre image with the English word to be learned. Thus, you might picture a dog with a very long chin. Suppost the next pair were *le livre* = the book. You might take as the keyword the word "lever" and picture a lever lifting a book.

The hypothesis here is that, in your subsequent readings in French, when you come across the French word (e.g., *le chien*) you now have two chances to remember the meaning of the word. You may, of course, directly remember its English equivalent. Failing this, however, *chien* may remind you of "chin," which, in turn, will evoke your original image of the dog with the long chin and, hence, the English equivalent.

Although the keyword method seems artificial, it has the endorsement of many researchers. In a comprehensive review, Pressley, Levin, and Delaney (1982) suggest that the keyword method surpasses all others in learning a foreign vocabulary. Furthermore, they say, people who use this method generalize to more natural use of the foreign language: they learn to read the language better than those who used other vocabulary-learning methods (e.g., repeated review of the word pairs). There is, however, one qualification. The method works best in one direction. Given the foreign language term (either in a vocabulary test or in reading a passage in that language), you readily remember the English equivalent. However, the keyword method does not appear to help with the reverse task. Given the English word, one does not recall the foreign language term any better than with other methods. In other words, the method helps you to learn to read in a foreign language but not to speak or to translate from English into that language.

It is worth reviewing, therefore, a second way in which visualizing may be used to enhance the learning of a foreign vocabulary. Although there is no formal research evaluating this method, it is one that I have used myself and have found to be effective. One can imagine saying the word in the presence of the object itself. For example, if you want to learn that the French phrase *le chien* means "the dog," you can say *le chien* and picture a dog. Use the phrase in a simple sentence that you know and imagine yourself in an appropriate situation talking, say, to a friend. Thus, you might say *"Regardez le chien,"* imagining yourself pointing a dog out to a friend, adding *"Le chien est noir* [black]," if that is the color of the dog you are imagining. If the next word-pair on your list is *le livre* = the book, you might picture yourself giving a book to a friend, saying *"Voici votre livre."* Or, to give yourself a review, you might imagine a dog carrying a book between his jaws and say *"Le chien porte* [is carrying] *le livre."*

Although the effectiveness of this second method is not established in formal research, it uses imagery, which we now know is generally effective for remembering. It should definitely be better than the usual flashcard, rote-learning method. It also has a certain naturalness to recommend it. We picture ourselves in situations similar to those in which we might one day use the words. We practice, in imagination, the way we might actually use the words if we were living in that foreign country.

This *practicing in imagination* has other uses that we will discuss later. For now we may note that Anderson (1980), in an important book on thinking, suggests that practicing in imagination is useful for other kinds of memory problems. He writes:

To remember an intention, imagine the situation in which you will have to carry it out and vividly imagine yourself carrying it out or imagine something associated with the intention. If you have to buy some soap on your way to the gym, imagine yourself walking to the gym and then turning off to go to the drug store, or imagine yourself walking into the gym and seeing a huge bar of soap there. To remember where you are putting something, imagine yourself wanting find it and then looking in the place where you are now putting it. (Anderson, 1980, p. 58)

In general, we are most likely to remember a future action (saying the correct word, making a purchase, locating an object) by rehearsing that action in the proper setting. Practicing the action in the *imagined* proper setting is an excellent substitute for practicing it in the real world.

As was emphasized earlier, intimate engagement has two properties: zest (giving energy and time) and seeing (visualizing). All the cases we have just discussed about aids to remembering have both of these properties. First, you actively engage the material. You do not just passively connect the words *"le chien* = the dog," but you make an effort: You think of a keyword, you picture a scene. You give more of yourself over to the learning. Second, you use your (inner) eyes—you visualize. If the problem is to remember, seeing is solving.

EXERCISES FOR INTIMATE ENGAGEMENT
(Appendix B contains additional answers.)

1. A dryer has two heat settings, Warm and Hot. When the switch is set to Hot, the machine normally feels much hotter than when it is set for Warm. One day you notice a change. Although the switch is set to Hot the dryer feels only warm to you. You check it out the next day and become convinced that Hot is producing only the same moderate temperature as Warm.

Q_1: **How do you think this dryer produces heat? (Hint: How do light bulbs and toasters produce heat?)**

A_1: It is likely that the heat is generated by passing electricity through a coiled wire.

Q_2: **What do you think is the construction that allows for the two settings?**

A_2: There could be two coils. When the switch is set on Warm only one coil is heated. On Hot both coils are heated.

Q_3: **What is the next step?**

A_3: After unplugging the dryer unscrew the back panel. Look for and check on those coils. Are there two? Is one broken?

2. You have a common, if unglamorous, problem. Your toilet is broken. You move the handle, which moves freely, but nothing happens. The toilet doesn't flush; that is, the water doesn't flow from the tank into the bowl.

Q_1: **Try to imagine the connection between movement of the handle and the resulting rush of water from the tank into the bowl. What must the construction be like?**

A_1: The handle must be connected by a chain or a rod to some sort of a stopper. Pulling on the handle lifts the stopper so that the water in the tank is released.

Q_2: **What do you think went wrong?**

A_2: The chain or rod between the handle and the stopper must have broken or fallen off the handle.

Q_3: **What action should you take?**

A_3: Remove the top of the tank and look inside. Verify your imagined construction. Do you see something like a broken chain?

3. A sleep research laboratory proposes to compare two brands of sleeping pills, brands X and Y, for their effectiveness. Ten men will be recruited who, for $20 per night, are willing to sleep in the laboratory every night for a period of six weeks. Each person will take one of the pills before going to sleep each night. He will take brand X for one week, then brand Y for the second week, brand X for the third week, and so on. (This will be counterbalanced, so that half the men will start with brand Y). Each

morning each person will rate how well he slept with a single number ranging from zero (slept terribly) to ten (slept soundly).

Q₁: **Can you visualize the experimental plan? (Externalize—Make a diagram showing who will receive what pills when.)**

A₁: After you have drawn your diagram, compare it to the one shown at the end of this problem.

Q₂: **How many total ratings will the researchers obtain?**

A₂: Ten people will each provide 42 ratings, for a total of 420 ratings.

The researchers approach a pharmaceutical company to fund the research.

Q₃: **How much money will the drug company have to allocate just for the research recruits?**

A₃: The ten subjects will each receive $20 per night for 42 nights. This comes to $8,400.

The drug company asks if the subject costs can be cut approximately in half. They ask, "Can five subjects be run? Or can the experiment be run for only three weeks?"

Q₄: **What is wrong with these two alternatives? What is a better compromise?**

A₄: Five subjects, or any odd number, is not elegant. Half the subjects are receiving pill X while the other half are receiving pill Y. Therefore, you would like an even number of subjects. Similarly, an odd number of weeks is not ideal. You would like each subject to receive pill Y for the same number of weeks that he receives pill X.

Q₅: **What is a better compromise?**

A₅: Have eight men participate for four weeks. Everything will be counterbalanced. The cost will be 8 * $20/night * 28 nights = $4,480.

			WEEK			
PERSON	1	2	3	4	5	6
1						
2						
3	X	Y	X	Y	X	Y
4						
5						
6						
7						
8	Y	X	Y	X	Y	X
9						
10						

4. Consider the following list of sixteen words in the Fredonian language and their English equivalents. Learn the odd-numbered pairs by using the keyword method (see pp. 35–36). Learn the even-numbered pairs by repeating them to yourself five

times each. About twenty-four hours after learning these pairs, take the test shown following Exercise 12. See how many of each of the two types of word-pairs you remember. Judge for yourself the effectiveness of the keyword technique.

 1. *vilnorim* = police officer
 2. *klavik*   = potato
 3. *volniky*   = ocean
 4. *dorbichel* = headache
 5. *copel*   = avenue
 6. *dipenik*   = trumpet
 7. *nassit*   = artist
 8. *bondor*   = sunset
 9. *pilchin*   = banana
10. *volikin*   = automobile
11. *pentalis* = monkey
12. *tibilis*   = carpet
13. *renfo*   = pencil
14. *sorbun*   = sugar
15. *digitum*   = painting
16. *rikin*   = mouse

5. A day or two after completing Exercise 4 try this one. Attempt to memorize the following list of words thusly: Go down the list once, one word at a time; use the pegword method (one-is-a-bun, etc., see pp. 32–35) for the words labeled with a "p"; learn the other words by repeating each one five times. Wait about twenty-four hours (try to avoid rehearsing the words during this time); then test yourself by writing down all the words you can recall. Which method yields better results?

  p1:   1. bicycle
         2. elephant
  p2:   3. carrot
         4. clarinet
  p3:   5. syrup
         6. lawyer
  p4:   7. basketball
         8. whistle
  p5:   9. computer
        10. dancer
  p6:   11. balloon
        12. palace
  p7:   13. cowboy
        14. turtle
  p8:   15. waiter
        16. violets
  p9:   17. umpire
        18. mustard
  p10: 19. handkerchief
        20. telephone

6. Begin with the square of a given number, n (e.g., let $n = 15$; begin with $15^2 = 225$).

Q_1: **How much must be added to that number (here, 225) to produce the next square ($16^2 = 256$)?**

A_1: In this example, 31 must be added to 225 to produce 256.

Q_2: **In general, that is, for any n, how much must be added?**

A_2: Derive the relationship for all n by building a function generating table. (After making the table, compare yours with the one shown in Appendix B.)

Q_3: **From studying this table, what is the relation between n and ($n + 1$)?**

A_3: The difference between the squares of two adjacent numbers, n and $n + 1$, is the sum of the two numbers, $n + (n + 1)$. Thus, in A_1, $31 = 15 + 16$.

Q_4: **Can you now prove algebraically the relationship between n^2 and $(n + 1)^2$?**

7. Bill J. has, he believes, a foolproof method for winning at roulette. He will bet 1 dollar on black. If he wins, he will again bet 1 dollar on black. If he loses he will double his bet and keep on doubling each time he loses, betting 1 dollar, then 2 dollars, then 4 dollars, and so on. Whenever he wins he will start again betting 1 dollar and will repeat the method. Bill says "sooner or later black is bound to win and then I am 1 dollar ahead." (*Note:* In roulette black and red come up randomly each close to 50 percent of the time. If you picked the winning color, you win exactly what you bet on that spin. If Bill is betting 8 dollars the first time that black comes up, he keeps his 8 dollars, and the house gives him 8 dollars).

Q_1: **Suppose Bill loses on the first n spins. What is the function relating A, the amount bet, to n, the number of the spin?**

A_1: A function generating table like the one used on page 20 will indicate that $A = 2^{n-1}$.

Q_2: **Why does Bill say that as soon as he wins (no matter at which spin) he will be 1 dollar ahead?**

A_2: Make up another function generating table, this one showing the total amount lost, T, after C consecutive losses. It will indicate that $T = 2^{n-1} - 1$.

Bill followed his system perfectly for eight spins. He won on the first and second spin and lost on the next six spins. After the eighth spin (his sixth consecutive loss), Bill declared that he was "wiped out," he had no money left.

Q_3: **How much money did Bill start with?**

A_3: Bill bet 1 dollar at spin 3, doubling up for the next six spins and losing consistently. He lost a total of 63 dollars, but 2 dollars were gained on the first two spins. He started, therefore, with 61 dollars.

8. Beth and Lisa, who had been math majors and roommates at college, meet on the street. Here is part of the conversation.

    BETH: YOU HAVE THREE DAUGHTERS? HOW OLD ARE THEY?
    LISA: THE PRODUCT OF THEIR AGES IS 36.
    BETH: THAT'S NOT ENOUGH INFORMATION.
    LISA: DO YOU REMEMBER OUR ROOM NUMBER AT COLLEGE? THE SUM OF THEIR AGES IS THE SAME AS THAT ROOM NUMBER.
    BETH: OF COURSE I REMEMBER OUR ROOM NUMBER, BUT THAT'S STILL NOT ENOUGH INFORMATION.
    LISA: MY OLDEST WISHES THAT SHE HAD A TWIN SISTER.
    BETH: OK. NOW I KNOW THEIR AGES.

Q_1: You want to figure out the ages of the three daughters. How do you begin?

A_1: Begin by *externalizing*. List all the possibilities that fit Lisa's first statement. (*Note:* Only whole years are intended; not years plus months or fractions).

Q_2: What was their room number? (*Hint:* Why isn't the information in Lisa's second statement sufficient?)

A_2: Of all the possibilities of three numbers that multiply to 36, only two have the same sum, that is, leave Beth still uncertain about the ages. That sum, 13, must be their room number.

Q_3: How old are the three daughters?

A_3: The only ages that fit with Lisa's three statements are 2, 2, and 9.

The following problems are not conceptually difficult, but demonstrate, nevertheless, the advantage of externalizing.

9. Four men, Ed, Fred, Jed, and Ted, are going to the bank. The black-haired fellow has 40 dollars. Jed has as much money as the other three together. Fred, who has 10 dollars less than Ted, would have had more, but he spent some of it to have his hair dyed blond. The bald fellow is broke. Altogether they have 80 dollars.

    What is the red-head's name? How much money does he have?

10. If Bill were twice as tall as he is today, he would be 10 inches taller than Tom. In fact, Tom is 15 inches taller than Bill. How tall is each person?

11. Four men own the following musical instruments: Matthew, oboe and bassoon; Hank, trumpet and flute; Jack, flute and clarinet; Bill, trumpet and oboe. If the bassoon is cheaper than the oboe, the trumpet is more expensive than the flute, the oboe is cheaper than the flute, and the bassoon is more expensive than the clarinet, who owns the most expensive instruments?

12. Smith, Johnson, and Cohen live in Brooklyn, Manhattan, and the Bronx (not necessarily in that order). They are flying to New York City in a jet whose pilot, copilot, and navigator are named Smythe, Jenson, and Kohn (again, not necessarily respectively). It is known that

    a. Cohen lives in The Bronx
    b. Johnson is deaf and mute.
    c. Smythe had a brief fling with the copilot's wife
    d. The passenger whose name sounds like the navigator's lives in Brooklyn. The navigator, however, lives in Manhattan.
    e. The navigator's next-door neighbor, one of the passengers, is a famous opera singer.

What are the positions of Smythe, Jenson, and Kohn?

Test for Exercise 4

For the sixteen Fredonian words that follow, write the English equivalent.

nassit
volikin
digitum
klavik
vilnorim
rikin
pilchin
tibilis
renfo
dorbichel
volniky
bondor
pentalis
dipenik
copel
sorbun

Compare the odd- and even-numbered words in Exercise 4. Which of the two methods produced better recall?

SPECIAL FEATURES

6

SPECIAL FEATURES OF THE PROBLEM SPACE

Researchers on problem solving occasionally study the effects of hints on solution behavior. A difficult problem is presented to the subject. When the subject appears unable to solve the problem, the experimenter provides a hint of some sort. The typical purpose of such research is to determine the relative effectiveness of different kinds of hints.

Consider, for example, a well-known problem-solving task studied by Maier (1931). Maier tied two strings to hooks in the ceiling about 15 feet apart. Each string hung down from its hook to a point about a foot above the floor. The strings were far enough apart that a person holding the bottom end of one of the strings and walking as far as he could toward the other, could not reach and take hold of the other. The situation is suggested in Figure 6.1. Except for a pair of pliers lying about and the experimenter standing with his pen and paper, the room was empty. The task Maier gave to his subjects was: tie the two strings together.

If, after several minutes had passed, the subject still had not solved the problem, Maier gave him a hint. Without saying anything he walked into one of the strings causing it to sway briefly. This event sometimes directed the problem solver toward a solution: attach a weight to one of the strings and start it swinging like a pendulum. The subject then tied the pliers to one of the strings, started it swinging, then went and took hold of the other string bringing it as close as he could to the still-swinging string. When that swung toward him, he caught it and was then able to tie the two strings together.

Our interest here is in the hint. By providing it, Maier gave his subject, who was apparently blocked, a new direction to go in—a new start in an otherwise baffling situation. Let us think of a hint in that way: It provides us with a new direction in the problem space when we

FIGURE 6.1   Maier's two-string problem. The two strings are hung from the ceiling far enough apart that a person holding one cannot reach the other.

are stopped and don't know how to proceed. Another example of this role of a hint would be if you were in a maze looking for the goal and came to a choice point with four paths going off in different directions. A knowledgeable observer might say, "try path B." He isn't telling you where the goal is but is suggesting how to start moving again. Thus, when you are stopped in a problem space, a hint suggests where and how you might move.

Suppose, however, that we're alone with a problem—there is no "knowledgeable observer" present (or if there is, we don't want him to give us any hints). Is there any way that we can tell ourselves where to start and how to move when we find ourselves baffled and blocked? For many problems there is. Frequently, there is a special feature in the problem space that serves as a useful guide. We as problem solvers must learn to to be sensitive to these features so that we may more readily locate them. These special features are the hints. This is the thesis of these next chapters. Special properties of the space can guide us through the problem. By studying examples in several problems we will, it is hoped, begin to learn what these features look like. We will learn, in short, how the material of the problem itself can give us hints. This chapter will deal with problems in which all that is required is a search of the space for its special features. The next chapter will deal with special features produced by systematically changing the problem.

For the first example, consider the elegant problem shown in Figure 6.2, called the "Lonely-8 problem. The task is to replace each X with a digit between 0 and 9, so that the result is a correctly solved problem in long division. Spend a few minutes now studying this problem to see, not merely if you can determine the solution, but how you started toward the solution. What was the first step you were able to take? Then, if you became stopped midway, what moved you further along? Questions like these will be the concern of this and the next chapter. For the Lonely-8 problem, my own answers to these questions will be presented later. Let me suggest that you try that problem now.

*   *   *   *   *   *   *   *   *

```
              X X 8 X X
    X X X ⟌ X X X X X X X X
              X X X
              X X X X
              X X X
              X X X X
              X X X X
```

FIGURE 6.2
The Lonely-8 problem. Substitute a digit between 0 and 9 for each X so that the result is a correctly solved problem in long division. (*Note:* Initial digits in a string are never zero.)

I want to postpone the analysis of the Lonely-8 problem. Consider, first, a new problem, the cryptarithmetic problem shown here:

$$
\begin{array}{cccc}
 & L & E & T & S \\
+ & W & A & V & E \\
\hline
L & A & T & E & R \\
\end{array}
$$

In this problem, each letter represents one of the digits between 0 and 9. The same letters, for example, the two A's, stand for the same digit; different letters take different digits. A solution is the assignment of digits such that the result is a correct addition problem.

Let's begin this problem together so that I can directly demonstrate the search for special features. Before we do so, however, it is useful to review an elementary property of addition. When you add a column of digits (in this problem we're adding four columns each containing two digits) if the sum is equal to or greater than 10 you must carry a 1 to the next column. We will indicate this carrying by parentheses, as (1).

Now, how shall we proceed? Where is the special feature in this problem space? Notice that the first column, $S + E = R$, consists of just three different letters—nothing special there. Similarly for $T + V = E$, $E + A = T$, and $L + W = A$, there is nothing unusual with any of these. What appears to be special?

What is that L in the answer doing all by itself, under a column without any letters? How can that be? That configuration is certainly a special-looking feature. Can you determine what L must be? If not, let's take a step that we will discuss systematically in Chapter 8: Let's ask the question under simpler conditions. Suppose the entire problem were

$$
\begin{array}{cc}
 & L \\
+ & W \\
\hline
L & A \\
\end{array}
$$

$L + W$ clearly add to a number greater than 9, to something in the teens. Of course! That L standing alone must equal 1. (L cannot be a 2; no two digits can add up to 20.) We can now write

$$
\begin{array}{cc}
 & 1 \\
+ & W \\
\hline
1 & A \\
\end{array}
$$

This result leads to the next step. We know that 1 + W must be greater than 9 (always keeping in mind that a (1) may possibly be carried from the preceding column). Therefore, W must be a large digit. Whether we carry (1) from the preceding column or not, W cannot be 7 or less. Can W = 8? Yes, but only if we carry (1) from the preceding column. Notice that if W = 8 (and we carry (1) from the preceding column), then the sum is 10 and A = 0. Can W = 9? Yes, but only if we do *not* carry (1) from the preceding column (since carrying a (1) in this case would make A = 1, which it cannot be because L = 1). If, therefore, W = 9 then A = 0. We may conclude, then, that W is either 8 or 9, depending on whether or not we carry (1), and that in either case A *must be 0.*

If we go back now to the original problem, we'll see that we have made some progress.

L	E	T	S		1	E	T	S
W	A	V	E	$\longrightarrow$	(8,9)	0	V	E
L	A	T	E	R	1	0	T	E	R

We've narrowed the task down to the three right-hand columns, although we are still a bit uncertain about W. Is there now something peculiar in these three right-hand columns? Is there a special feature? Yes, that 0 in the third column. Usually, adding a 0 to something doesn't change it. How then can E + 0 = T? It can only mean that a (1) is being carried from the preceding column. T must be exactly (1) more than E. Let's write that third column as an equation, starting with the (1) that is carried:

$$(1) + E + 0 = T$$

Can T be part of a two-digit number (i.e., in the teens)? Only if E is 9, then T would be 0. But we saw that A is already 0, so E = 9 is ruled out and T is not part of a two-digit number. Most important, therefore, a (1) is not carried to the next column. What does that say about that next column? Right! W = 9.

Let's stop here and review our strategy. To get started we looked for a special feature in the space and found the L standing alone. That permitted us to make some progress. Then we noted the 0 in the third column (the only special feature in the three right-hand columns) and that led us to see a simple relationship. This strategy exemplifies the procedure advocated in this chapter. A scan of the problem space will sometimes reveal an unusual feature. This feature is frequently a "hint," a good place to start exploring. Incidentally, it is probably no coincidence that the zero in the third column was useful. The 0 is one end of the series of digits. According to a principle discussed in the next chapter (called "Look at the Extremes"), the ends (or extremes) of dimensions are frequently special features.

We will not continue with this cryptarithmetic problem here. Those of you who want to complete it on your own will need a piece of information that I have so far neglected to give you: S = 7. The entire problem is worked in Appendix A.

We will consider another cryptarithmetic problem later. For now I want to return to the Lonely-8 problem in Figure 6.2. Do you remember (or, better, have you jotted down) your attempts at solution? How did you begin? What features of the problem permitted you to make progress? Those are the features that we will be emphasizing.

Before we look for these special features, however, we will do well to remind ourselves of the language and rules of long division. Consider the problem as it is presented in Figure 6.3. The three digits at the left (the divisor, abbreviated DIV) are multiplied in turn by each digit in the answer (the quotient). The product of (divisor * quotient-digit) is written appropriately underneath the number divided into (the dividend) and is subtracted. In Figure 6.3 the products have been labeled PROD 1, 2, and 3 for ease of reference. Following each subtraction, successive digits from the dividend are carried down to the difference until the resulting number is larger than DIV. The next product is then obtained, and so forth. Since all this is familiar, let us go on.

There are several special features in this problem. For example, PROD 1 was not placed under the first three digits but under the second three. What does that mean? Perhaps the most unusual feature in the space, and the one that offers a promising beginning, is the fact that PROD 2 is a result of multiplication by a known digit, 8. Let us start, then, with PROD 2. Where does that beginning lead? We see that multiplying 8 by DIV, which is a three-digit number, produces—a

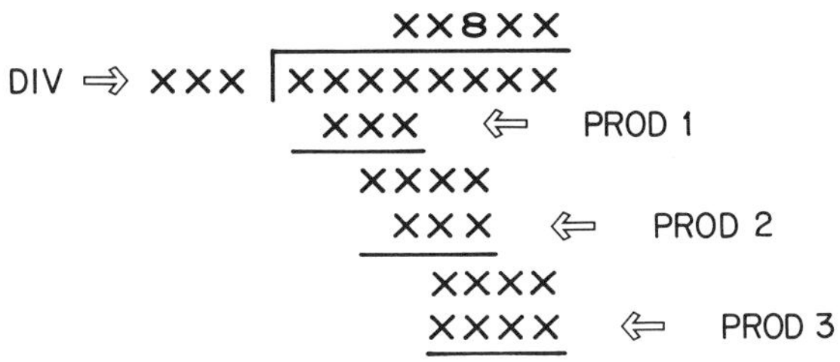

FIGURE 6.3 The Lonely-8 problem again, with some of the terms labeled.

three-digit number. How can that be? Only if DIV is a relatively small three-digit number. Can DIV be a number in the 200's? No, for 8 * 200 would yield 1,600, and we would have a four-digit product. DIV, therefore, must be a number in the 100's. The leftmost digit of DIV, in other words, must be a 1. By similar reasoning, actually, we can know that DIV must be less than 125 since 8 * 125 = 1,000, a four-digit number. DIV, therefore, is a number between 100 and 124, and PROD 2 is some number between 800 (8 * 100) and 992 (8 * 124).

What is the next special feature to consider? Let us stay with PROD 2 for the moment. It is between 800 and 992. Look at PROD 2 in Figure 6.3; there's something peculiar about it. It is subtracted from a four-place number but yields only a two-place result, that is,

$$
\begin{array}{cccc}
x & x & x & x \\
- & 8 & x & x \\
\hline
& & x & x
\end{array}
\qquad \text{or} \qquad
\begin{array}{cccc}
x & x & x & x \\
- & 9 & x & x \\
\hline
& & x & x
\end{array}
$$

How can that be? The only combination for which this can hold (the reader can check this out by trying different sets of numbers) is

$$
\begin{array}{cccc}
1 & 0 & x & x \\
- & 9 & x & x \\
\hline
& & x & x
\end{array}
$$

where, from the second column, a (1) is "carried" to the 9. Therefore, DIV * 8 > 900 so that DIV ≥ 113 (and is not greater than 124).

Where shall we now turn? As we indicated, there are several special features in this problem, any of which would repay investigation. Let us here consider next PROD 3. First, it has a couple of special features. It is the only product with four digits, the others have only three; also, when subtracted, it yields all zeroes; that is, it is identical to the number it is subtracted from. Furthermore, that number is related to PROD 2 (it is the answer produced after subtracting PROD 2), a number about which we already have some information.

We know that multiplying DIV by 8 yields a three-digit number that is greater than 900. However, multiplying DIV by the final quotient-digit yields PROD 3, a four-digit number. This can mean only that that final quotient-digit is larger than 8. Specifically, it must be 9. Since DIV is between 113 and 124, PROD 3 must be between 9 * 113 = 1,017 and 9 * 124 = 1,116.

The problem, with the new knowledge that we have gained, is shown in Figure 6.4. Let us leave, now, the problem of the Lonely-8

```
               XX8X9
DIV  ⇒   1XX │XXXXXXXXX
             XXX
            ─────
            1OXX
             9XX     ⇐   PROD 2
            ────
            1XXX
            1XXX     ⇐   PROD 3
            ────
```

FIGURE 6.4   The Lonely-8 problem with several of the digits filled in.

(which is no longer so alone). For those of you who wish to continue, I'll point out a couple of other special features: the 1 beneath PROD 2 and the fact that two digits must be carried down before we can obtain PROD 2. Can you find others? The complete problem is worked in Appendix A.

The next problem is fairly familiar, but it serves an important function: it expands the meaning of the concepts "problem space" and "special features". Here is the problem:

A man leaves his camp by traveling due north for 1 mile. He then makes a right turn (90 degrees) and travels due east for 1 mile. He makes another right turn and travels due south for 1 mile and finds himself precisely at the point he departed from, that is, back at his campsite. Where is the campsite located (or where on earth could such a sequence of events take place)?

In the previous problems, the problem space was the space of the givens. Thus, we studied the presented configuration of the crypt-arithmetic problem and of the Lonely-8 problem, looking for anything unusual in that configuration. In the cryptarithmetic problem, it was the extra letter leftmost in the answer. In the Lonely-8 problem, it was the 8, itself, and the zeroes resulting from subtraction. These were all in the presented materials. In the present problem the givens are in the statement of the problem itself, and that all seems straightforward. Where shall we look for special features? Let's broaden the concept of problem space to cover more than the givens. Here the problem space will include not only the givens but all the possible solutions. Specifically, it will include all the places in the world from which the man might start his trip. In the current problem we have an infinite range of solutions—all the possible places on the earth. It is among these that we want to look for special features. For all of you, I'm sure, two types of special features come to mind: the equator and the poles. It is intu-itively obvious that everyplace else on earth is like every other place in that, for any of these, the givens would be impossible—the camper would end up some distance east of his starting point.

Consider first the equator. Could the campsite be located on some point of this central line? No, because the camper would end up exactly 1 mile east of the campsite. How about the North Pole? No, because it is given that he traveled north. From the North Pole one can travel only south. How about the South Pole? That leads to the path shown in Figure 6.5 and is, indeed, the solution.[3]

For the final problem in this chapter let us consider the well-known cryptarithmetic problem shown earlier, in Figure 2.1 (p. 6). This problem is to be solved according to exactly the same rules as the cryptarithmetic problem just given: Each different letter represents a different digit, and so on. Here it is given that D = 5; therefore, T = 0 and a (1) must be carried to the next column. What special features do we see in this problem? First, we see that in columns 2 and 3, the same letter is repeated: L + L = R and A + A = E. We can make some small progress with these facts, but they will not carry us too far. Specifically, we know that R must be odd. Whenever a digit is added to itself, the result is an even number (2 + 2 = 4, 3 + 3 = 6, etc.), but L + L has (1) carried from the preceding column. The sum of (1) + L + L, therefore, must be odd.

A second special feature concerns the leftmost column. We know one of the letters (D = 5). Also, the sum must be no greater than 9, or else there would be another letter, a letter standing alone, at the left of the answer (compare the L in the answer of the preceding crypt-arithmetic problem). Thus, R must be greater than 5, and, from (1) + L + L = R, it must be odd. This leaves exactly two possibilities, 7 or 9.

Any other special features? Yes, a most important detail. In the second column from the left, we have O + E = O. Something (here, E)

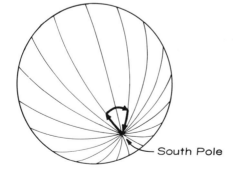

FIGURE 6.5
A view of the South Pole showing how, by traveling north, east, and south, you can arrive back at your starting point.

South Pole

---

[3]There are other solutions to this problem. For the purposes of our illustration, the North Pole solution was dismissed correctly but too casually. While the North Pole itself is not a solution, its configuration, its "specialness," produces nearby solutions.

added to a number produces the same number. How can that be? One easy answer is that E = 0, since 1 + 0 = 1, 2 + 0 = 2, and so on. Unfortunately, this won't work because it is already given that T = 0. How else can O + E = O? Suppose a (1) were carried from the preceding column. In such a case E could be 9. We would have (1) + O + 9 = O (and carry a (1) to the last column), that is, (1) + 1 + 9 = 1 (carry (1)), (1) + 2 + 9 = 2 (carry (1)), and so on. Therefore, E = 9 and (1) is carried to the leftmost column. Recall, now, that in that column R was either 7 or 9. Since E is 9, R must be 7. The left column, then, has (1) + 5 + G = 7, and G must be 1. These results are shown in Figure 6.6.

The rest of the problem is straightforward and won't be carried out here (but see Appendix A for the entire problem). Our lesson, again, is that the unusual configuration in a problem space is frequently a hint indicating a starting point. Here the unusual configurations were the repeated letters in a column, especially in the second column from the left. Notice that in the various problems the unusual feature took a different form. It was the L standing alone, it was the digit 8, it was the repeated letters. There is no predicting in advance what it will look like. You must survey each problem on its own terms to see what features are special. Anything unusual, however, is worth exploring.

	(1) (1) (1)
D O N A L D	5 O N A L 5
+ G E R A L D $\Rightarrow$	1 9 7 A L 5
R O B E R T	7 O B 9 7 Ø

FIGURE 6.6 Part of the solution to the cryptarithmetic problem.

Section III
(continued)

SPECIAL
FEATURES

7

GO TO
THE EXTREMES

In the preceding chapter the special feature was located simply by searching the problem space. It might have been the space of the givens (as in the cryptarithmetic and the Lonely-8 problems) or the space of the solutions (as in the travel problem), but nothing more than a study of this space was needed. In this chapter and the next, we will consider special features that are produced by manipulation of the space. It is occasionally worthwhile to transform the space in standard ways, to work on a special case of the problem. Sometimes th's produces the solution directly. More frequently, the change helps us to gain insight into the structure of the problem, an insight that applies to the original problem. The prescriptive principle that we will discuss here is: *Look at the extremes.* This rule covers two kinds of transformations. In one, reviewed in this chapter, we look at the extreme limits of the problem space. In the other, considered in the next chapter, the extreme that we consider is that of simplicity—we will transform the problem to a simpler version.

Let us demonstrate going to the extreme limits with a few problems.

Two flagpoles are standing, each 100 feet tall. A 150-foot rope is strung from the top of one of the flagpoles to the top of the other and hangs freely between them. The lowest point of the rope is 25 feet above the ground. How far apart are the two flagpoles?

Stop here. Take some time to solve this problem. Jot down a note describing how you would (or did) solve it. See if your method agrees with the analysis that follows.

            *   *   *   *   *   *   *   *   *

A commonly drawn representation of the problem is shown in Figure 7.1. The problem seems to call for a brute force attack: get out our books on analytic geometry and, from the formulas, work out the spatial relationships. Let us first ask, however, whether there isn't a simpler approach. The suggestion here is: look at the extreme possible conditions of the problem. First, let's look at the largest extreme. How

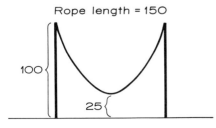

Rope length = 150

100

25

FIGURE 7.1
A standard representation of the flagpole problem.

far apart can the poles be? What does the situation look like at that point? Well, the poles can be 150 feet apart. The rope is then taut with the central point 100 feet above the ground—clearly not related to the solution. Consider, now, the other extreme: How close together can the poles be? Of course, they can be right next to each other (0 inches apart). The rope then would be folded in half 75 feet on a side and its low point would be 25 feet from the ground. Clearly we have the answer.

Another problem involving the same principle comes from Martin Gardner (1981), a leading writer on recreational mathematics. Gardner's version went something like this:

> As a spaceship was cruising through space, it passed along a large flat, disklike ring of dust. The navigator determined that the ring was bordered by two perfectly concentric circles. Its shape, in other words, was like a phonograph record with a large opening in the center. The captain declared that it would be of scientific value to know the area of the disk.
>
> "Well," said the navigator, "the ship had cruised alongside the disk on a straight line that crossed the outer circle at point *X,* was tangent to the inner circle at *Y,* and crossed the outer circle again at *Z.*" The navigator further announced that in going from point *X* to *Z* they had traveled exactly 200 miles.
>
> "That's all well and good," said the captain, "but what is the area of the disk?"
>
> "I'm not sure I can obtain that," said the navigator. "We do not know the radii of the inner and outer circles."
>
> A lieutenant standing nearby, who knew the principle *use your eyes, externalize,* drew a picture of the disk. This is shown in Figure 7.2. The captain glanced at it and remarked, "Say, that reminds me of a theorem I once learned in geometry. The area of the band between the two circles is determined by the length of that chord *X–Z.*"
>
> "You mean," checked the lieutenant cautiously, although a certain excitement was in his voice, "that given that the length of *X–Z* is 200 miles, the area of the disk is a constant regardless of the sizes of the two circles?"
>
> "Right," replied the captain.
>
> The lieutenant immediately announced the area of the band.

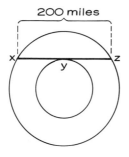

200 miles

FIGURE 7.2
The ring of dust and the 200-mile path, *XYZ,* taken by the spaceship.

How did he do it? What is the area of the band between the two circles? The only additional information you need is the well-known mathematical fact that the area, A, of any circle of radius r, is given by

$$A = \pi r^2$$

Notice something else. The theorem the captain referred to says that if the disk looked as it does in Figure 7.3, the area would still be the same.

FIGURE 7.3
Another possible representation of the ring and the 200-mile path.

See, now, if you can figure out how the lieutenant was able to solve the problem so quickly. After you try to solve it, write a note describing your method, the way you went about it.

*   *   *   *   *   *   *   *   *

In tackling this problem, let us follow our new rule and study the problem at the extremes. Let us first make the radius of the inner circle as large as possible. This is the direction taken in Figure 7.3. We quickly realize that there is no limit. No matter how large the inner circle is, we can always have an outer circle such that the chord X–Z is 200 miles. (We can see, incidentally, why it is plausible that the area of the disk must be constant. As the radius of the ring increases, the distance from the inner to the outer circle decreases; compare Figures 7.2 and 7.3. How about the other extreme? We can imagine making the disk smaller until the inner circle becomes so small as to be indistinguishable from a point at the center of the outer circle. At that point, the disk has the appearance shown in Figure 7.4 and the answer

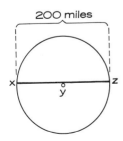

FIGURE 7.4
The representation of the ring at the other extreme.

is obvious: The area of the disk is the same as the area of a circle whose radius is 100 miles. In other words,

$$A = 3.1416 * 100^2 = 31,416 \text{ mi}^2$$

As before, the problem is solved at an extreme.[4]
Here is a related problem.

> You have a large, solid sphere of gold. A cylinder of space is "bored" through this sphere, producing a ring (see Figure 7.5). The length of that cylindrical line is 6 inches. You want to know how much gold you have left in the ring. Specifically, What is the volume of the ring? (It is known that the volume, V, of any intact sphere is given by the formula,
>
> $$V = \pi D^3 / 6$$
>
> where D is the diameter of the sphere.)

Note that no information is given about the dimensions of the original sphere. It could be as large as the earth, in which case the ring would be approximately 25,000 miles long (the length of the equator), 6 inches wide, and paper thin; or it could be the size of a bowling ball, producing a thick ring with a thin, 6-inch long tube of space running through the center. The fact that we can vary the size of the sphere in this way seems to imply that the answer, the volume of the resulting ring, is independent of the original sphere size. To put it another way, the answer should be the same no matter what the original sphere size.

Again, try at this point to solve this problem. After you solve it—or try to solve it—write a note describing your method, the way you went about it. The solution will be found in Appendix A.

FIGURE 7.5 Two views of a sphere that has been drilled through, producing an inner cylinder of space 6 inches in length.

*   *   *   *   *   *   *   *   *

[4]The theorem referred to by the captain, that the area of the disk depends only upon the length of the chord and not upon the radii of the circles, is not difficult to prove. Try it for yourself. The proof will be found in Appendix A.

The next problem not only affords another opportunity to use our principle, *look at the extremes,* but provides an interesting contrast with another popular approach to problem solving.

As shown in Figure 7.6, a circle with a 1-inch radius has a rectangle inscribed in one of its quadrants. What is the length of line *k*?

This problem was first presented by the Gestalt psychologist Wolfgang Köhler as a demonstration of the importance of "seeing" the problem differently, of having "insight" into the structural relations inherent in the problem. While I am sympathetic with that view of problem solving, here it leaves us unguided. It advises us to be sensitive to the problem structure. Aside from that, however, the new way of seeing the problem, the happy insight, occurs mysteriously. In contrast, our current maxim (look at the extremes) is at least a procedure for generating a reasonable determination of the answer.

In the preceding problem, the size of the sphere was unstated, with the implication that the answer was independent of sphere size. Here the dimensions of the rectangle are unstated, with the implication that *k*, the length of the diagonal, will be the same for *any* such inscribed rectangle. Thus, in Figure 7.7, the rectangle is narrower than in Figure 7.6. Since the problem asks only for *k* without specify-

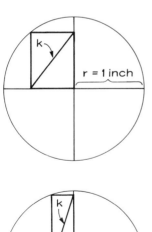

FIGURE 7.6
A rectangle inscribed in a quadrant of a circle whose radius is 1 inch. What is the length of *k*?

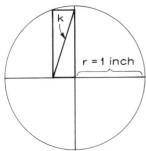

FIGURE 7.7
The same problem as in Figure 7.6 with a more extreme rectangle.

ing the rectangle, presumably the diagonal is the same for any such inscribed rectangle.

Let us now see if we can solve the problem by going to an extreme. What happens as we make the rectangle still taller and thinner, so that the two longer sides start to become the same line? As this happens, the two sides approach the length of the radius. *The diagonal, also, will approach the length of the radius.* Thus, at the extreme, the diagonal equals the radius. If our presumption is correct, that k is the same for all such rectangles, then the answer is that k equals the radius, that is, $k = 1$ inch.

It is interesting to contrast this method of arriving at the solution with that proposed by Köhler. He suggested two steps. First, we must be prompted by the bright idea of drawing into the rectangle the other diagonal. Second, we must recognize that that other diagonal is the radius of the circle. His demonstration is superior to the one I've proposed since it does not require any assumption about the invariance of the solution for different rectangles. In fact, it *proves* that that assumption is correct by determining the answer for any arbitrarily selected rectangle. In that sense, it is certainly a better solution.

As we noted, however, the difficulty with Köhler's solution is that it depends upon inspiration, upon getting the bright idea. It must occur to us to draw in the other diagonal. Where does this inspiration come from? Köhler provides no guides. Our look at the extremes, on the other hand, is a rule that we can take out and apply like a tool from a toolbox. For the three preceding problems, the flagpole, the disk, and the sphere problems, it is not clear that "inspiration" could serve you better than application of the rule.

There is another consideration. In the sphere problem and the diagonal problem our procedure was valid only on the assumption that the answer was constant for all values of the unspecified givens. If this assumption were not correct, then the answer would be complex. It would be a mathematical function of the critical dimension of the figure, that is, of the diameter of the sphere and of the size of the rectangle. The problem would then belong in the realm of mathematical textbook proofs rather than in casual, semirecreational discourse. In other words, there is a tacit understanding that the answer to such problems is simple.

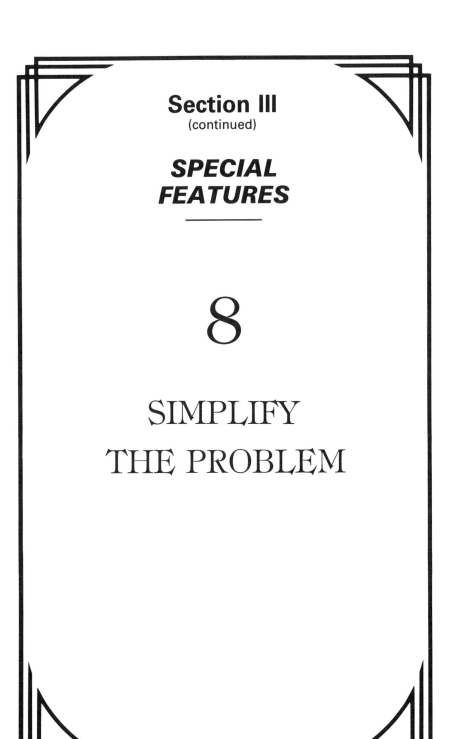

Section III
(continued)

SPECIAL
FEATURES

8

SIMPLIFY
THE PROBLEM

We have just considered the special features produced when the problem was moved toward an extreme. That extreme was a limit, a boundary, of one of the dimensions. The nature of that dimension depended on the problem. Now we will consider variations along a particular dimension, the dimension going from complex to simple. The extreme of interest here is the simplest case.

Consider this example: A friend proposed the following stunt. He said, "Write down a long number, about seven or eight digits in length. Do not show it to me." I wrote the number labeled A in Figure 8.1. He continued, "Write the number in reverse." I did and he added, "You now have two numbers, the original and the one in reverse. Write the smaller of the two numbers underneath the larger of the two, and subtract one from the other." Figure 8.1 shows my number in reverse (labeled B) and the subtraction carried out.

A ⇒ 9 3 7 4 6 3 6 1
B ⇒ 1 6 3 6 4 7 3 9
———————————————
7 ⑦ 3 8 1 6 2 2

FIGURE 8.1
A digit-guessing problem. The number B is the reverse of the number A and, being smaller, is subtracted from it. It is possible to deduce the digit that is circled just from hearing the other digits in the answer.

The instructions continued: "Circle one of the digits in your answer. Circle any digit other than a zero. After you have done this, read aloud to me the remaining digits. That is, read all the digits in your answer except the one that you circled. Read them in any sequence." For the problem shown in Figure 8.1 I read "1-2-2-3-6-7-8." After reflecting for no more than two seconds he said, "You circled a 7." Figure 8.2 shows another such problem, for which he would, after hearing the other digits, inform me that I circled a 6—or whatever else I had just circled.

How did he do this? Or, more to our present concern, how can we figure out how he did this? This is the problem we will consider here: How shall we proceed to determine his secret? One brute force method is to write out a great many of these problems and hope that some pattern will emerge. I don't recommend this in quite that way; there will be too much variation from problem to problem to see the relationships. A hint, however, on how to proceed is in his vagueness about the length of the original digit string. It obviously could be any length. The problem should work, therefore, with digit strings of very short

B ⇒ 9 2 3 5 9 8 8
A ⇒ 8 8 9 5 3 2 9
———————————————
3 4 0 ⑥ 5 9

FIGURE 8.2
Another digit-guessing problem. Whereas the number, A, in Figure 8.1 has eight digits, this one has seven.

lengths (e.g., two or three digits). Let's try several two-digit lengths. A few examples are shown in Figure 8.3

$$
\begin{array}{cccc}
41 & A \Rightarrow 83 & A \Rightarrow 75 & 51 \\
A \Rightarrow 14 & 38 & 57 & A \Rightarrow 15 \\
\hline
27 & 45 & 18 & 36 \\
\end{array}
$$

FIGURE 8.3   Several digit-guessing problems where the starting number, A, consists of two digits.

What pattern do we see in these answers? Consider one property: they are all multiples of 9. Is that fact relevant to the longer strings, the ones shown in Figures 8.1 and 8.2? Not really. Our friend surely doesn't know *all* strings of all lengths that are products of 9. Is there any other property common to the answers in Figure 8.3? Yes, each answer adds to 9; that is, 2 + 7 = 9, 4 + 5 = 9, 1 + 8 = 9, and 3 + 6 = 9. Thus, there seems to be something odd about this procedure of writing a number, reversing, and subtracting: The digits in the answer add to 9. You could actually do the trick yourself now using two-digit numbers. The digit circled would always be 9 minus the remaining digit.

You might explore now the answers for three- and four-digit numbers. I recommend that to you. After doing that, let's return to the original problems shown in Figures 8.1 and 8.2. They obviously don't sum to 9; they're too large. However, they sum to multiples of 9 (7 + 7 +-- + 2 = 36, 3 + 4 + -- + 9 = 27). The omitted circled number is the one needed to bring the sum to the next higher multiple of 9. Voila! You are now ready to mystify your friends.

Note the procedure we followed in our detective work. We were given a problem in a complex (seven or eight digits) form. We solved the problem by studying analogous, *simple* forms. This is the rule proposed here: Simplify the problem; look at the simple extreme.[5]

The next example is the Tower-of-Hanoi problem of which a typical display is shown in Figure 8.4. This problem is particularly important for a single reason: It has been explored in several experiments

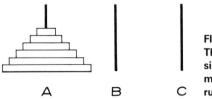

A   B   C

FIGURE 8.4
The Tower-of-Hanoi problem. The six disks on pole A are to be moved to pole C according to the rules described in the text.

[5]The method of determining the omitted number can be streamlined a bit. See if you can improve on it.

during the past decade (for the more recent research, see Kotovsky, Hayes, and Simon, 1985). The problem is presented to the solver more or less as follows:

> As you see, six disks are all stacked on pole A. Your task is to have all the disks stacked in exactly the same way on pole C. There are the following restrictions on how the disks are to be moved: (1) You must move only one disk at a time; (2) the disk must be moved from one pole to another (it may not be temporarily placed elsewhere); (3) it must never be placed on top of a smaller disk. You may begin.

Figure 8.4 shows a tower with six disks. The exact number of disks used may vary from problem to problem.

The typical way in which this is studied is to record the moves that the problem solver makes. Sometimes he or she is asked to think aloud, and the verbal reports are also recorded. These and the record of movements are analyzed in an effort to determine the various strategies used by different people. Clearly, these studies yield descriptive principles, principles that tell us how, in fact, people approach this problem. Our concern here, in contrast, is with prescriptive principles: How *should* one approach such a problem?

In this section we are considering one of these prescriptive principles: Look at special features of the problem space; more specifically, look at the extremes; still more specifically, look at the simple extreme. What this means here is turn away from this six-disk problem. Solve the problem first for a two-disk problem (illustrated in Figure 8.5). Solve it for both forms of the two-disk problem; that is, first move the two disks from pole A to pole C then move them from A to B. (These two-disk problems are simple enough that you can probably do them in your head. You may, however, want to *externalize*, to cut out a few disks of different sizes to study this Tower-of-Hanoi problem.) When the two-disk problems are mastered, try the three-disk problem (see Figure 8.5). What insights start to occur?

Suppose that for both the two- and three-disk problems, the task is to shift the stack to pole C. You will have noticed that for the two-disk problem the first move requires putting the top disk on B; for the

A   B   C   A   B   C

FIGURE 8.5   A two- and three-disk version of the Tower-of-Hanoi problem.

three-disk problem, the top disk must be moved to C. What general rule does this suggest? Notice, also that both the two- and three-disk tasks have as a preliminary goal (sometimes called a subgoal) moving the bottom disk to C. This means that all the disks above the bottom disk must first get onto B. For the three-disk problem in Figure 8.5, we must first arrive at the configuration shown in Figure 8.6. But that is equivalent to the two-disk problem, where we must get the top two disks onto B. What rule does that suggest?

As you see, working at this simple version of the problem can provide you with an understanding of its fundamental properties. This knowledge will transfer to the original six-disk problem which you can probably now do without a misstep. We see again that a complex problem is solved by first exploring a simple version.

It may strike you as a strange recommendation, that to solve a problem most efficiently you should turn away from that problem temporarily to work on another (a simple) version of that problem. Would not the time spent on the simple version be better spent—or at least as well spent—on the more complex version? At least, you might argue, we would then be moving toward the solution of interest (e.g., for the six-disk problem).

Here some laboratory research comes to our support. An Australian psychologist, John Sweller, has demonstrated what he calls the *sequence effect*. The general procedure involves giving two groups of subjects the same set of related problems. One group receives the set in the order going from the simplest to the most complex, the other group receives the set in the reverse order, with the complex problem presented first (sometimes, for this group, the complex problem is not followed by any other).

A typical experiment (Sweller, 1980a) went as follows: College students were presented with a starting number and were told that they must convert it into another number in a fixed amount of moves using only certain arithmetic operations. Specifically, they were told that the starting number was 8 and that they must convert this to 15 in exactly six moves (neither more nor less) with the allowable operations of multiplying by 2 and subtracting 7. The solution consists in alternating multiplication by 2 and subtraction by 7, with the first

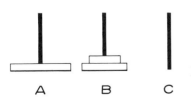

FIGURE 8.6
A subgoal, or necessary stage, on the way to solving the three-disk problem.

move being multiplication. Thus, starting with 8 you would go 8 * 2 = 16, 16 − 7 = 9, 9 * 2 = 18, 18 − 7 = 11, 11 * 2 = 22, 22 − 7 = 15.

Sweller presented this problem to two groups. One group (complex) simply received this problem; the other group (simple to complex) first received two simpler problems (e.g., convert 8 to 9 in two moves using those two operations). On the average, the complex group required over 406 seconds to solve the one problem; the simple to complex group required only 97 seconds to solve the same (the complex) problem *and only 192 seconds for all three problems.* Sweller has demonstrated this effect with a variety of problems. Even problems that people normally fail at can be solved after practice on simpler versions (Sweller, 1980b).

To generalize this result to the Tower-of-Hanoi problem, I'd predict that people, after studying the two- and three-disk problems for 5 minutes, will perform the six-disk problem in nearly the minimum number (63) of moves, requiring approximately 2 minutes. Thus, a total of about 7 minutes will be used. People working only on the six-disk problem, without the detour to the simpler versions, will make many more moves than the minimum number and will require considerably more than 7 minutes. Furthermore, exploring the simpler problem permits you to have insight into the structure of the task,so that you can readily solve any Tower-of-Hanoi problem. People who worked only on the six-disk problem have difficulty if they are next given the five-disk problem. One's performance working only on the six-disk problem is so much trial and error that one transfers little learning over to other forms of the problem. Working with the simple versions, on the other hand, should provide insights that are useful for any version of the problem.

The mathematician Polya, in an early but still pertinent essay on how to solve mathematics problems (Polya, 1957), also advocated this principle of simplify the problem. Here is one of his examples:

A rectangular-shaped room is given whose dimensions are A, B, and C. What is the length, x, of the diagonal from the lower right-hand corner in the front to the upper left-hand corner in the back? The diagram is shown in Figure 8.7.

If you do not find this an easy problem, that is, if you do not see immediately how to proceed, then, suggests Polya, use this rule: "Look at the unknown! And try to think of a familiar problem having the same or a similar unknown" (Polya, 1957, p. 9). Polya refers to a "familiar problem" where we speak of a simpler problem. In practice, familiar problems will tend to be simpler than the novel, difficult problem. In this particular case, we are asked to find the diagonal of this three-dimensional figure. What simpler (or familiar) problems have

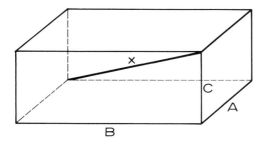

FIGURE 8.7 Express the length of the diagonal, *x*, in terms of the known lengths *A, B,* and *C.*

you faced with a similar unknown? Well, you all have, I am sure, learned to find the hypotenuse of a right triangle whose sides are known. Also, knowing this, you can find the diagonal of a two-dimensional rectangle whose sides are known. Review that information. Is it relevant to the present problem? The answer will be found in Appendix A.

    *   *   *   *   *   *   *   *   *

The importance of working with simpler versions of a problem was also emphasized by Wickelgren (1974, pp. 157—166) who provides these examples:

(1)—You have 24 coins that look alike. With the exception of one counterfeit, they are all made of gold and weigh exactly the same. The "bad" coin is either heavier or lighter than the others, you do not know which. You also have available an old-fashioned balance scale. What is the minimum number of weighings you must make in order to locate the bad coin?

    *   *   *   *   *   *   *   *   *

This problem is interesting in that there are two ways you can simplify. First, suppose it is known that the bad coin is, specifically, heavier. Second, consider the problem with three coins. Of course, you may combine both types of simplification, that is, begin with three coins, one heavier. Determine the minimum number of weighings for these simple problems; then return to the more complex version.

(2)—You are given 10 stacks of what should be 10 gold pieces each. Each gold piece weighs two ounces. Unfortunately, one stack contains 10 counterfeits, each coin weighing only one ounce. You have a bathroom-type scale, one that reads out the weight put on by printing it on a card. The problem: Determine the counterfeit stack with a single weighing

    *   *   *   *   *   *   *   *   *

If you are baffled by this last problem, try it for three stacks with three coins each. See if you don't find this reduced version easier to think about. These problems are discussed in Appendix A.

There seems to be no question but that, by simplifying a problem, we increase our chances of solving the original. To the many examples given in this chapter we could add others. (Try the anthropologist problem given on pp. 17–18 by assuming that the anthropologist and her husband meet only one other couple; the function generating section in Chapter 3 essentially recommends working systematically with simplified versions.) Evidently, the simple version more readily permits us to achieve insights into fundamental properties of the problem. This was clear in the opening digit-guessing problem and the Tower of Hanoi.

Why is that? Why are we more likely to see the solution with three gold coins than with twenty-four gold coins? In Chapter 3, when we discussed the virtue of externalizing information, we reviewed evidence that our conscious mind is limited in its capacity. I believe that that limitation underlies this advantage of simplifying. We must visualize more in a complex problem than in a simple problem. For example, we must visualize ten stacks of ten coins as opposed to three stacks of three coins. The six-disk Tower of Hanoi is confusing even when it is physically in front of you, whereas you can do the two-disk version in your head. Because, with the simpler version, we need to visualize fewer things, we can employ more of our cognitive capacity for solving the problem.

Why, then, is the principle *simplify the problem* effective? It helps us to overcome a limitation inherent in the way that we humans handle information.

EXERCISES FOR SPECIAL FEATURES

(Appendix B contains additional answers.)

1. In the following cryptarithmetic addition problem it is given that O = 0 and I = 1.

$$
\begin{array}{r}
F\ L\ Y \\
F\ O\ R \\
\underline{Y\ O\ U\ R} \\
L\ I\ F\ E
\end{array}
$$

Q₁: What special features do you see that will get you started?
A₁: The third column: It has two letters that are the same (the F's) as well as a 0 and a 1.
Q₂: What is the value of F?
A₂: F must be 5, and a 1 is carried from the preceding column.

2. A man built a rectangular house such that each side had a southern exposure. One day a bear lumbered past the house. What was the color of the bear?

3. Consider the following drawing.

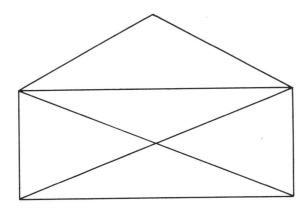

Q₁: Can you draw the figure in one continuous movement, without taking your pencil from the paper and without tracing any part of the path two times?
A₁: Yes, by starting at the lower left-hand corner of the rectangle.
Q₂: For each of the pairs of figures shown at the top of the following page, one can and one cannot be drawn in one continuous movement. For each pair indicate which one can be drawn.

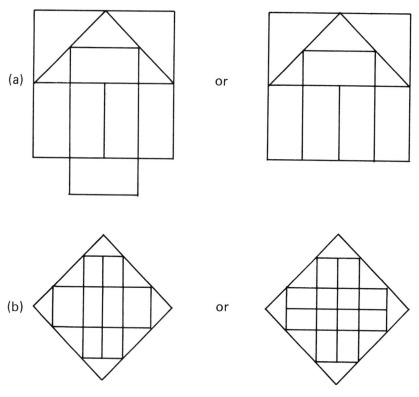

A_2: Both left-hand figures can be drawn in one continuous, nonoverlapping line; the ones on the right cannot.

Q_3: **How would you determine the principles that underlie (1) the decision as to where to begin drawing these figures and (2) the method for constructing them?**

A_3: Construct and study several simple versions such as the following. Check out your insights on the more complex figures. The principles are described in Appendix B.

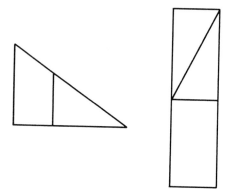

4. A car goes on a 20,000-mile trip. The tires, including the spare, are rotated every 4,000 miles, so that the five tires were used for an identical number of miles.

Q_1: **For how many miles was each tire mounted on the car, in use?**
A_1: Consider a simple extreme and externalize. The trip was divided into five units and the tires rotated after each unit. Suppose the car went 5 miles and the tires were rotated every mile. Make a chart showing how each tire would be placed (i.e., on the car or in the trunk) each mile. Apply the resulting answer to the original problem.

Q_2: **Is there another way of simplifying the problem?**
A_2: Yes. Focus on a single tire, the spare. Each tire was the spare for exactly one of the 4,000-mile units. It was mounted on the car, therefore, for the other four 4,000-mile units.

5. Jo announces: "I have more than 999 books."
Jean says: "No, Jo! You have fewer than 1,000 books."
Mary says: "Jo has at least 1 book."
Only one of these statements is true. How many books does Jo own?

6. In discussing the Tower of Hanoi, we said that the minimum number of moves in which the six-disk problem can be solved is 63 (see p.66). Can you determine how that was arrived at? Can you determine the minimum number for a five-disk version? Can you derive the equation relating the number of disks to the minimum number of moves? *(Hint:* Simplify and externalize, that is, make a function-generating table.)

7. A stranger comes to a mountain inn and tells the owner that he must stay there and wait for a friend who will come sometime within the next twenty-one days. Unfortunately, he says, he has no money. He produces, however, a chain of exactly twenty-one gold links and convinces the innkeeper that the links are of the purest gold. He offers to give in payment one link per day. The innkeeper agrees that a gold link is easily worth a day's food and lodging, but only if the link is intact. A cut link, he says, is nowhere nearly as valuable as an intact link. He does not want to end up with twenty-one cut links. The visitor then works out an arrangement where, giving the innkeeper one more link each day, he will cut the minimum number of links. What is the smallest number of links that he must cut? *(Note:* "Swapping" may take place; for example, on the tenth day the guest may exchange a string of ten links for the nine links the innkeeper is holding.)

Q_1: **What is a good way to proceed?**
A_1: Consider this problem, first, for a smaller number of days and links. Suppose, for example, the problem involved five days and five links, or seven days and seven links, and so on.

8. A large city has close to 100,000 children in the eighth grade. The mean IQ of this population of eighth graders is known to be 100. In a genuinely random way you are to select fifty of these children for a study of educational achievements. The first child tested has an IQ of 150. What do you now expect the mean IQ will be for the whole fifty-child sample? In other words, do you still expect the mean IQ of the sample to be about 100? Or do you expect it to be slightly greater than 100?

Q_1: **What is a good way to gain insight into this problem?**
A_1: Look at the extreme. Assume that the sample size is not fifty but two; that is, only two people are to be randomly selected, the first of whom has an IQ of 150. What do you expect the mean IQ of this sample to be? Is the answer not clearer in this form?

9. A man starts striking a bass drum every 2 seconds.

Q_1: **From drum beat 1 to drum beat 60 how much time has elapsed?**
A_1: If your answer is 2 minutes (or 120 seconds), think again. Simplify the problem to determining the elapsed time between the drumbeats 1 and 2, between 1 and 3, and so on. In effect, make a function-generating table.
Q_2: **Now, what is the answer to the original problem?**
A_2: (60 − 1) * 2 = 118 seconds.

Section IV

LATERAL THINKING

9

DON'T BE BLIND

A great deal of evidence, some of which we will review here, suggests that when people try to solve a problem, they typically employ a standard strategy. That is, they follow some habitual mode of responding. Most of the time this strategy (or the habit) is appropriate to the problem: The person who holds that strategy solves the problem faster than does someone who does not. Occasionally, however, a mismatch occurs; the strategy is not appropriate to the particular problem at hand. This leads to a baffling aspect of problem solving: The person acts as though he or she were blind to the solution.

This temporary functional blindness has been demonstrated in a variety of ways in the laboratory. It is dramatically illustrated, however, in a couple of incidents that were reported to me.

> (1)—A woman was with her baby son in the living room of her house. The infant was sitting on the rug peacefully sucking a rubber nipple as the mother was tidying the room. Suddenly the boy swallowed the nipple which lodged in his throat; he started gagging and crying. The alert mother sat the child up and slapped his back, hoping that the blow would dislodge the obstruction. It didn't work. She started to become frantic and thought of hitting the child's back while holding him upside down. She called for help to her sister who was in another room of the house. The sister came in, heard in a rush of half-sentences the problem and what the mother wanted to do. Going over to the choking baby she saw a string coming out of his mouth. She pulled on the string and out came the nipple. Happy ending.

The mother, fixed on this notion that hitting the back was the way to dislodge something stuck in the throat, literally failed to see the string; she was functionally blind to it.

> (2)—A fellow was sitting alone in the passenger side of his own car, a two-seater sports model. The car, standing on a slightly inclined street, started to roll backward. The man tried to get around the stick-shift to get his foot onto the brake pedal but the movement was awkward, difficult, and slow. Before he could succeed the back of the car banged into a pole.

What here reflects functional blindness? Immediately to his left, between the two seats, was the hand brake. So strong was the fellow's habit, his "set," toward using the foot-brake pedal that the hand brake was utterly blocked from his consciousness. It never occurred to him to pull up on the handle just to his left. He was blind to that possibility.

These anecdotes describe the functional blindness of people in urgent situations—there was danger and time was short. Functional blindness, however, is a more general phenomenon. We do not require these special circumstances to see it. Research psychologists, using situations in which there is no stress or urgency, have succeeded in demonstrating the effect. They have labeled it with a variety of terms: einstellung (a German term meaning "set" as in "set in his ways"), set, rigidity, functional fixedness, and functional blindness. An early and well-known demonstration was given by Luchins (1942), who presented people with a series of water-jar problems. A typical water-jar problem goes as follows:

> You have three jars, one that holds 11 quarts, one that holds 9 quarts, and one that holds 4 quarts (referred to as the 11, 9, and 4 jar, respectively). How can you obtain exactly 6 quarts of water?

One solution is to fill the 11 jar, pour from it and fill the 9 jar, leaving 2 quarts in the 11-jar. Fill the 4 jar and pour it into the 11, thus producing 6 quarts. If we label the 11, 9, and 4 jars as A, B, and C, respectively, then the solution may be symbolized as $A - B + C$. Luchins presented a series of such problems to students of various ages. A sample series is seen in Figure 9.1. The problem we just discussed is shown in the top row of that figure. Before reading on, try to solve the remaining ten problems. Do them in the sequence 1 to 10.

＊　＊　＊　＊　＊　＊　＊　＊　＊

You have no doubt noticed that you ran into a dead-end on Problem 10, that a habitual mode of solution suddenly didn't work. You had to back up and go off in a new direction. It probably took you longer to solve Problem 10, although it has a very simple solution. All the other problems can be solved by the pattern B-A-2C. (For example, problem 1 is solved by filling the 127 jar (B), pouring from it and filling first the

	Jars			
PROBLEM	A	B	C	OBTAIN
DEMONSTRATION	11	9	4	6
1	21	127	3	100
2	15	90	4	67
3	14	163	25	99
4	18	43	10	5
5	9	42	6	21
6	20	59	4	31
7	14	36	8	6
8	23	49	3	20
9	7	20	4	5
10	28	76	3	25

FIGURE 9.1　A series of water-jar problems. The demonstration problem is described in the text. Solve the remaining problems in the sequence 1 to 10.

21 jar (A) and then the 3 jar twice (2C); this leaves 100 quarts in the B-jar.) Problem 10, however, is not solved by that but by the simpler pattern A-C. About three out of four people (adults as well as children) go through the long solution and learn that it fails. They review the problem again and only then do they see the simpler solution (sometimes people first retry the long solution thinking that they had made an arithmetical error).

A more surprising result concerns Problems 7 and 8. Both of these can be solved in the usual way (B-A-2C), and most of you undoubtedly solved it that way. Did you notice, however, that there was also an easy way (A-C) to solve those problems? Or were you functionally blind to that solution? Again, about 75 percent of people fail to see the easier solution.

Sweller and Gee (1978) took this last demonstration even further. At Problem 7 one of the jars held the target amount. They might, for example, present 37, 80, and 3 as A, B, and C, with the task of obtaining 37 quarts. Most of the people tested used the B-A-2C method!

Another striking demonstration of set came from my own laboratory (Levine, 1971). A person is shown a deck of 3-inch × 5-inch cards on each of which is typed just two letters: A and B. On half of the cards, the A is on the left side of the card with B on the right; on the remaining half, the two locations are reversed. The cards do not vary in any other way. There are 50 of each of these two types. The deck has been thoroughly shuffled, so that the two types of cards are randomly distributed throughout. The person is given the following instruction: *Go through the deck slowly one card at a time, choosing (and saying aloud) at each card one of the two letters.* The experimenter says "correct" or "wrong" for each choice according to a preselected solution. (The learner has been told to try to be correct as often as possible.) Some typical solutions might be (1) always choose the letter that's on the right side of the card; or (2) choose alternate sides (i.e., choose the letter on the right on the first card, the letter on the left on the second, then right, then left, etc.); or (3) choose according to some more complex sequence of positions, for example, first choose the letter on the left, then right for the next two cards, then left once, and right once then start over (i.e., go L-R-R-L-R repeatedly); or (4) choose A all the time; or (5) choose some sequence of the letters (e.g., go A-A-B-A-B repeatedly). From his own choices and the correct-wrong feedback from the experimenter, the problem solver can figure out what the solution is.

The problem of interest here is the one with the simplest solution: Choose A all the time. If you're an observer watching the experimenter present this problem to a student you might hear something like: "A" "correct"; "B" "wrong"; "A" "correct"; "A" "correct"; "A" "correct"; "B" "wrong"; and so on. The problem couldn't be easier. Any self-respecting monkey learns a similar problem (for food, of course) in perhaps ten to twenty trials (i.e., choices). College students typically learn it in about three trials.

How can we demonstrate einstellung with this simple problem? Can we arrange the conditions such that the student, who is typically eager to do well, is functionally blind to this pairing of "A-correct" and "B-wrong"? The anwer is yes. Suppose the student is led to expect that the solution will be a complex position sequence (such as "choose the letters according to the pattern L-L-R-L-L-R-R-L-R; then start over"). In other words, suppose he is primed to look for one of these complicated sequences, but in fact the solution is the simple "choose A." In such a case he will fail. He will appear to be saying A and B randomly.

How did we produce such functional blindness? Specifically, we constructed six decks of such cards and gave the subjects a series of six problems. Each of the first five problems had as its solutions a complex position sequence. Students typically became good at solving such problems; that is, they quickly figured out the position sequence and responded correctly thereafter. After the fifth problem, the experimenter said, as was said after each of the other problems, "That ends that problem; here's a new one." The student then was handed a new (the sixth) deck. For this sixth problem, the experimenter used the easy "choose-A" solution. In this case, almost all the students failed: They chose A only half the time throughout the entire problem. This problem lasted for one hundred trials. That is, the students said "A" fifty times and heard "correct"; they said "B" fifty times and heard "wrong." Nevertheless, they failed to see the simple solution. When asked at the end of the problem what the solution was, they almost always said that they thought it was some complicated position (L-R) sequence.

Let's review one more variant of einstellung, first described by Duncker (1945). He showed that people become so attached to the particular function of an object (e.g., shoes are used to protect one's feet) that they fail to see other uses to which the object might be put. Consider these situations: You are working at your desk when a wind blowing through an open window at the other end of your room starts to scatter several papers on your desk. How do you both hold the papers down and get to the window to shut it? Would it occur to you to use your glasses or your wallet as a paper weight?

You want to hang a picture in your office. You not only brought the picture, but you purchased special nails that should not damage plaster. Here you are ready to hang the picture when you realize that you don't have a hammer. Would it occur to you to use your shoe as a hammer? Duncker demonstrated that people frequently fail to solve a problem when the solution requires new functions for objects. He called this "functional fixedness." It is clearly a special case of einstellung.

Scanning these several examples, we see that we become functionally blind under fairly predictable circumstances. It happens when our behavior is dominated by routine or custom. Strong habits, previously successful strategies, and routine functional applications prevent our seeing obvious alternative strategies and functions. The question of concern in this book, of course, is what can we do about this? How can we prevent ourselves, in critical problem situations, from becoming functionally blind?

There are two types of answers to this question. One involves a point of view, an awareness that we have about problems; the other deals with specific techniques. We will discuss the role of awareness here. The specific techniques will be reviewed in the next chapter.

The first contribution to reducing einstellung is, then, awareness. What do I mean by this? The knowledge you have just gained, that fixation on one (incorrect) type of solution might happen, that you as a human being are vulnerable to such restricted thinking, should help you. Luchins ran some conditions with the water-jug series where he first told the people "don't be blind." He advised them to be flexible in the way that they went about solving the problems. The instruction was helpful. More of the people who had received such instructions found the simple solution on the critical problems (Problem 7 and 8 in Figure 9.1). In my own research on the "choose A" problem, I never specifically tried to instruct people in this way. Nevertheless, some revealing comments were made. A few people (about one in five) do solve that final, critical problem. When asked about it afterward one of these people who solved said, "We had just read about Luchins's experiment in my psychology course. I thought of that while doing this." Another said, "I was looking for a trick. Psychologists do things like that." Thus, the awareness of the possibility that the solution might lie elsewhere made it easier to break out of the set, to locate the solution.

The moral of both Luchins's and my experiments is that it helps to know about einstellung. This awareness can alert you, even while you're using a tried and true strategy, to other possibilities. The noted problem-solving theorist, Edward de Bono (1969, 1972) has formalized the consequences of this awareness very nicely. A conventional attack upon a problem he calls *vertical* problem solving. We unthinkingly have a preconception about how a problem should be solved and try to work forward with it even though we may be up against a hidden wall. He recommends instead *lateral* problem solving. See the problem in a new way. Come at it from a new direction. Don't just keep digging away at the wall; see if you can't sneak around it. He gives these examples:

(1)—He had returned from a trip on a wet icy night, arriving at the same airport from which he'd left and where he'd parked his car. Going out to the parking lot in the freezing rain, he saw that several people were having trouble because their car-door locks were frozen—the key wouldn't turn in the lock. Like the others he first tried heating the key by lighting matches but was having no success, in part because the wind kept blowing out the flame. Then he changed his direction entirely. Obviously, water had gotten into the lock and had frozen. He remembered that alcohol has a lower freezing point than water. Alcohol, therefore, might melt the ice. He took from his luggage a bottle of duty-free liquor that he had bought and poured a bit of it into the lock. In a moment the key turned easily.

(2)—He was staying alone in a country cottage and needed to iron a shirt, but no iron was available. He could, of course, have gone into town to buy one (the vertical approach, here wasteful of time and money). He was able, however, to find another type of solution: He heated up an available frying pan, put it into a paper bag and comfortably ironed the shirt. Note how this particular instance of the "lateral" approach entailed overcoming functional fixedness (frying pans are to fry things in).

(3)—An ambulance on a mountain road found itself behind a large flock of sheep. The driver sounded the siren and gently nudged the rearmost ram, but it was useless. The mountain embankments prevented the sheep from getting out of the road. Between the baaing of the sheep, the siren, and the driver shouting at the shepherd it was a din. Finally, the shepherd raised his hand to signal the ambulance driver to stop the vehicle. When it had stopped he turned the sheep around and led them back past the ambulance. In a minute the vehicle had a clear, unobstructed road. (This last example is close to the old vaudeville line, "Don't raise the bridge; lower the river." Here it is "Don't get the ambulance past the sheep; get the sheep behind the ambulance.")

Have you caught the spirit of lateral thinking? Even while working on the straightforward approach, you have to be alert to other possibilities, to solutions that come from a different angle.

These examples conclude our introduction to the topic of *einstellung*. In this we concentrated on demonstrations of the phenomenon. Although I haven't yet discussed specific techniques for avoiding this strange functional blindness, we did see that the very awareness of its possibility helps. Simply knowing about einstellung and about its converse, lateral thinking, should start you toward being a more flexible problem solver. The next chapter will supplement this initial advantage with some specific techniques for avoiding einstellung.

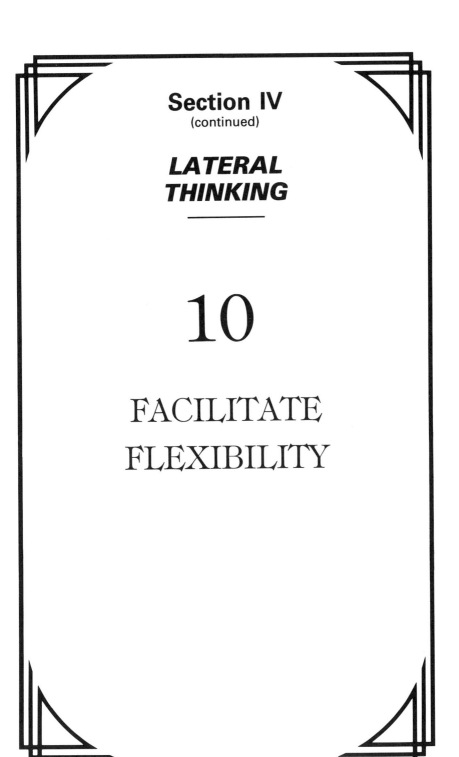

*LATERAL
THINKING*

10

FACILITATE
FLEXIBILITY

The several examples in the preceding chapter (the car lock is stuck, the shirt needs ironing, etc.) describe problems that arise suddenly and that affect a single individual. They are the sort of problems that might occur to you or to me at any time. However, most of the writing on flexibility in problem solving deals with problems that tend to be less acute. They are problems such as "How can I build a better mousetrap?" There is no urgency. You can take weeks or longer to think about and to solve the problem. Furthermore, several people can work on the problem simultaneously. They may work competitively or in a group, cooperatively. My favorite in this category is perhaps the clearest example of lateral problem solving. It also comes from de Bono (1969).

> A new skyscraper was built and the offices quickly rented. Within a few weeks a defect became obvious. There weren't enough elevators in the building to accomodate all the traffic. The owners of the building received a steady stream of complaints about the long wait for an elevator. Engineers and architects were called in and estimates were obtained of the cost and inconvenience of installing additional elevators. The estimates were depressingly high. One of the consultants, however, thought laterally and found a simple solution. Mirrors were installed on every floor near the elevators. People waited just as long but no longer found it boring. They had an interesting distraction (presumably themselves, but possibly also viewing the crowd, flirting, etc.). The number of complaints dwindled.

The second class of problems, then, tends to have solutions which can be thought about at one's leisure. We've just seen that the distinction between vertical and lateral thinking applies here. The awareness that one should not be rigid (think only vertically) but should be flexible (i.e., think laterally) should enhance one's ability as a creative problem solver. However, authors on this topic have a few specific techniques to recommend.

BRAINSTORMING

This is probably the best known of the techniques. Alex Osborn (1963), who is credited with its development, has trained hundreds of executives and engineers in its uses. The technique is applicable to any but, perhaps, the most acute problems. Brainstorming is frequently done by problem solvers in groups although individuals can certainly engage in it. A group of people interested in a specific problem are brought together. The problem is reviewed and solutions are requested. Two fundamental rules guide the search for the solutions.

The first and, perhaps, primary rule is that criticism is not allowed. Take any proposed solution, no matter how far-fetched, and write it down. It is easy to be critical of novelty, especially of other people's novel suggestions. However, nothing inhibits wide-ranging, flexible, lateral thinking like a critical, judgmental atmosphere. Don't judge. Even the crudest ideas are to be respected. The brilliant critic, who immediately sees the flaws in every suggestion, does not belong here. Neither does the bureaucrat who, comfortable with his routine, is afraid of change. One must feel free to be "lateral," to search for strange and wonderful ideas.

This attitude of *don't judge* is so important that I want to elaborate upon it. A positive equivalent is *respect crude ideas*. The human intellect seems to move naturally toward shaping, improving, streamlining. Clocks began as huge crank-and-lever objects, requiring frequent rewinding, and losing minutes of accuracy each hour. One can almost hear a fifteenth-century grouch complaining: "Clocks are useless. They keep slowing up and always need to be tended. They are more trouble than they're worth." Over the years, however, clocks have become streamlined, moving toward the contemporary wristwatch, automatically energized, accurate for months. Many inventions around us reflect this evolving process. Consider how television sets have gradually changed over the last forty years. From 6-inch screens with green-and-white blurry images they were designed and redesigned into 25-inch pictures in brilliant color with sharp-edge lines.

This step-by-step refinement can also occur within an individual problem. Here are two examples from my own experience.

(1)—In the middle of a project I needed to cut a rigid wire, about one-eighth of an inch in diameter. I looked for the wire cutter around my workbench but it was missing. Now what? How do I cut the wire and get on with my project? The following sequence took place over the next couple of minutes.

a. I remembered how, as children playing in the street, we would cut a piece of twine by rubbing it back and forth over the sharp edge of the curb. Could I do something like that with this wire? (This is the crude idea. It sounds foolish, but I didn't dismiss it. I actually looked around for a sharp edge.)

b. I next thought of *constructing* an edge, one that would be sharp enough to do the job. I could lock into the vise a hacksaw blade with the teeth sticking up above the vise. That way I could rub the wire back and forth over the teeth. I reached up to get a loose blade hanging near my hacksaw

c. "Wait a minute!" thought I. "Let's reverse this. Let's clamp the wire into the vise, take the hacksaw, and cut the wire. That, of course, was the natural way to do it. The crude idea became transformed, step by step, into a proper solution.

(2)—Two business partners, owners of a pet shop specializing in exotic animals, were discussing how to improve sales. They both agreed that many people are uneasy about buying these pets because of their own ignorance. People are afraid that they will do something wrong and possibly harmful to the animal. Partner A said "I know. With each animal purchased let's give away one of the books describing everything about the animal. We can play that up in our advertising." (This is the crude idea.) Partner B, who hadn't read Osborne or this book, immediately rejected it. "Are you crazy? Those books cost us six dollars apiece. We would be losing half the profits on the sale." Nevertheless, partner A stayed with the idea. First, he shopped around for less expensive books. Finally, he realized that the entire book, with photos and interesting facts about the animal, wasn't necessary. All that was needed was the section on the care and feeding of the animals. He wrote this out and again approached his partner, who now became more receptive. They had a printer make up a handsome pamphlet on the care and feeding of exotic animals and gave these out free, at a cost to themselves of less than one dollar each.

Moral: Don't be quick to reject "crazy" ideas. Live with them, explore them, refine them. This first rule is at the core of brainstorming.

The other important rule is that quantity is important. At the start of brainstorming, you should search for and express as many ideas as possible. Generate a good long list—without, remember, censoring. Only after a large set of alternatives is generated does the critical work begin. Even in this phase, where suggestions will start to be eliminated, each item on the list should be treated respectfully, looked at in a variety of ways, seriously explored. As we have seen, a clumsy idea may evolve into an elegant solution. Some ideas, inadequate by themselves, may be combined with others on the list to yield a useful solution.

An interesting feature of brainstorming is that it can be practiced like a skill. Osborne suggests several exercises, many of which serve as practice in overcoming functional fixedness (see pp. 77–79). We might call it *novel function practice*. Osborne asks, "How many uses can you think of for a brick?" You might try this now. Imagine that you own a brick-making factory. To stimulate sales you want to advertise all the ways that bricks might be used. Make as long a list as you can. Remember, do not censor. After you have finished, read on.

*   *   *   *   *   *   *   *   *

Most people begin by listing all the things that they could build out of brick: build a house, build a retaining wall, a shed, a barbecue, for example. Those are all within the traditional functions of a brick. Did your list include any "exotic" uses?

Consider these: a doorstop, a paperweight, an anchor, making brick sculptures and collages, weights for weight lifting, a new track event—the "brick put"—warming sheets on a cold night (these last two courtesy of Adams, 1974). This should give you the idea of how lateral thinking can be practiced. You can start over with other objects (novel uses for paper clips? for a paint brush? etc.). See if you can break away from the traditional functions of objects.

The remaining techniques appear on the surface to be different from brainstorming and from each other. However, they have an underlying common function. The aim of each of them is to stimulate novel approaches toward the problem. They are, in other words, direct strategies for flexibility in solving any problem.

THE INTERMEDIATE IMPOSSIBLE

This is a phrase coined by de Bono (1969) to describe a method that he pioneered. When you are blocked on a difficult problem, he suggests that you deliberately think of a clearly impossible solution. Let your mind play freely with it. He proposes that that will frequently lead to a novel and real, feasible solution. Thus, the *impossible* solution is *intermediate* between the problem and the ultimate solution. Here are some examples.

(1)—The loading and unloading of ships is uneconomical. The ship must sit dockside, it and its crew inactive, for the hours or even days it takes to unload. A concern for this problem makes one look for more efficient unloading systems. Perhaps one could make better use of cranes and other unloading equipment, or of the longshoremen. Instead of these obvious and well-explored possibilities, let's think, suggests DeBono, of something semifantastic. For example, suppose we think of unloading the ship while it is still at sea coming toward the port. What does that suggest (after you get past the image of the cargo being dumped into the sea)? Perhaps the ship could be redesigned so that most of the unloading preparation could be done while the ship is still at sea. Perhaps longshoremen could be flown aboard by helicopter and, while the ship was still traveling toward the port, could organize the cargo into specially designed containers. When the ship reached dockside the prepared cargo would then be all ready for unloading. One would need only to transfer it to the proper truck or train. Thus, the "wild idea" opens the way to new classes of solutions.

(2)—The city council of a port city learns that a new, efficient type of commercial ship is being used, but that it can't come into their city. The reason is that the main bridge spanning the river is a few feet too low. The new ships can't quite clear it. It appears that a major source of revenue will be lost to the city. One class of solutions is to raise or rebuild the bridge, and much thought would be expended on that. Remember the joke "Don't raise the bridge; lower the river?" Absurd, right? But let your imagination play with absurd possibilities. In this case, let's mull over "lowering the river." Perhaps the state government would be interested in shunting part of the river for an inland canal, or for a lake. Would it be cheaper to build locks to control water level than to replace the bridge? The point is that this absurd notion of "lowering the river" leads to a new class of potentially feasible solutions.

(3)—A factory on a river takes in pure water flowing past and dumps out polluted water. Of course, it is not the factory but the people downstream who suffer from the pollution. An intermediate impossible solution would be to put the factory downstream of itself so that the management would feel the effects of its pollution. That's silly, of course. However, this in turn led to the suggestion of simply exchanging the location of the intake and outlet pipes. Put the intake water pipe of the factory downstream of the outlet, pollution-discharging pipe. The factory could now monitor directly the amount of pollution it was producing.

RANDOM ASSOCIATIONS

This refers to another method proposed by de Bono. It helps, he suggests, to get a fresh start on a difficult problem by juxtaposing with it a word randomly chosen from the dictionary. He gives this example:

Suppose that you are an engineer trying to solve the problem of noise in your city. The vertical approach, of course, is to impose fines on people who make noise, who honk car horns, whose cars have defective mufflers, etcetera. Now let's follow de Bono's suggestion and randomly select a word from the dictionary. Suppose that the word chosen is "anthracite." Reflect on it. Let your mind roam freely between the word and your problem (here, reducing noise pollution). Anthracite comes from under the ground. What does that suggest? Perhaps traffic can be routed underground. Perhaps relaxation centers for quiet activities (libraries and the like) can be provided underground. Another direction: Anthracite is black, which suggests the absence of light. We have eyelids and pupils to protect ourselves automatically against bright light. The ears, however, have nothing like that. Perhaps we could invent similar kinds of ear protection (e.g., muscle-controlled or sound-operated flaps). Again, new classes of potential solutions come into being, more alternatives than if we focused only on how to stop people from making so much noise.

ANALOGIES OR METAPHORS

William J. J. Gordon, in a movement called Synectics, adds another technique for generating novel solutions: Look for analogies or metaphors (Gordon, 1961). In his writings he tends to favor biological analogies. As he puts it, "Biological perception of physical phenomena produces generative viewpoints." He cites these examples: A major problem of underwater construction was solved when Brunel observed a worm tunneling into timber. The construction of a tube as the worm moved suggested the method for underwater tunneling. Alexander Graham Bell studied the workings of the human ear and saw that a light membrane moved a relatively heavy set of inner bones. He used this idea of a membrane causing vibrations in heavy objects in his design of the telephone.

Gordon describes the application of biological analogy during an active problem-solving session with this example: A group was trying to design an energy-efficient roof. They considered the possibility of having a roof that would automatically change in brightness. It would be white in the summer and black in the winter. The white would reflect the rays of the summer sun and would reduce the need for air conditioning. In winter the black would absorb heat and would, therefore, reduce the cost of keeping the house warm. What sort of material would change like this? Here are excerpts from a dialogue among five people, A, B, C, D, and E. Note how the opening question begins a search for a biological analogy.

A: What in nature changes color?

B: A weasel—white in winter, brown in summer; camouflage.

C: Yes, but a weasel has to lose his white hair in summer so that the brown hair can grow in. . . . Can't be ripping off roofs twice a year.

B: Okay. How about a chameleon?

D: That is a better example because he can change back and forth without losing any skin or hair. He doesn't lose anything.

A: A flounder must do it the same way.

E: Do what?

A: Hell! A flounder turns white if lies on white sand and then he turns dark if he lands on black sand . . . mud.

D: By God, you're right: I've seen it happen! But how does he do it?

B: Do you want an essay?

E: Sure. Fire away, professor.

B: Well, I'll give you an essay, I think. In a flounder the color changes from dark to light and light to dark. . . . This is how the switching works: in the deepest layers of the cutis are black-pigmented chromatophores. When these are pushed toward the epidermal surface, the flounder is covered with black spots so that he looks black. . . . When the black withdraws to the bottom of the chromatophores then the flounder appears light colored.

C: You know, I've got a hell of an idea. Let's flip the flounder analogy over on to the roof problem. . . . Let's say we make up a roofing material that's black, except buried in the black stuff are little white plastic balls. When the sun comes out and the roof gets hot the little white balls expand according to Boyle's law. They pop through the black roofing vehicle. Now the roof is white . . . just like flounder, only with reverse English. Is it the black-pigmented part of the chromatophores that come to the surface of the flounder's skin? Okay. In our roof it will be the white-pigmented plastic balls that come to the surface when the roof gets hot.*

Person B was obviously a biological consultant. Notice how person C takes his biological description and transforms it for solving the roof-design problem.

SLEEP ON IT

The final technique for overcoming set or einstellung is, perhaps, the most widely recommended. Authors as different as Osborne, who focused upon industrial-corporate problems, and Wickelgren, who wrote on the solving of mathematics problems, make the same recommendation. When you are absolutely blocked on a problem, when none of the techniques seems to work, turn away from the problem. Do other things. The problem-solving process seems to be aided by the sheer passage of time—the technical term is *incubation*.

A problem resists solution because we have the wrong approach; we are thinking vertically. The recommendation is that we put the problem aside and become involved in other activities. This frequently has one of two results. The first is that the solution will later occur to us when we least expect it. It is as though the mind has been unconsciously working on the problem while we have been going about our daily routine. The second effect of taking a break is not only that the problem-solving process "incubates," but that our mind has changed when we return to the problem. We are less dominated, controlled, by the incorrect set we had several hours earlier. We are now more likely to think of new approaches. So, if you are frustrated by a problem, if you have engaged it intimately but nothing comes—stop. Come back to it later. This is a particularly powerful recommendation if you're work-

*Gordon, W. J. J. (1961). *Synectics*. New York: Harper. By permission of the author, 121 Brattle Street, Cambridge, Massachusetts.

ing on a problem in the late evening. Sleep on it. The mind seems to be more flexible in the morning. Many is the math problem that was impossible for me to solve at night that, the next morning was seen to be transparently simple.

This ends our discussion of einstellung. We have reviewed two methods for overcoming these effects of "set." One is the collection of techniques (brainstorming, taking the intermediate impossible, using analogies, incubation) just enumerated. The other is to be aware in any problem situation of the risk of einstelling. This means that even as you pursue a particular strategy with diligence, you stay alert to other possibilities, to more far-out, lateral solutions. Be flexible. Don't be entirely fenced in by past habits and strategies.

De Bono (1972) considers this attitude of flexibility so important that he has generalized it from problem solving to all of life. An approach to life in which you think imaginatively with a willingness to explore new ideas he calls *PO thinking* (from, I believe, the letter pair in words like supPOse, POssible, hyPOthesize—words that imply tentativeness). He contrasts this with YES-NO thinking, which he characterizes as logical, critical, and dogmatic. The addition of PO thinking to YES-NO thinking, he urges, will lead not only to better problem solving, but to a generally more creative life.

EXERCISES FOR LATERAL THINKING

(Appendix B contains additional answers.)

1. A circular cake is shown at the right. With a single cut you can easily divide the cake into two equal parts (see the dashed line in the figure). You can also divide the cake into four equal parts with two cuts by making the second cut at right angles to the first.

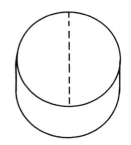

Q_1: **Can you, with three cuts, divide the cake into eight equal parts?**

A_1: Yes, but you must stop thinking about making another diameter across the top of the cake.

Q_2: **How else can you cut it?**

A_2: Slice it sideways, through the center of the cylindrical part of the cake.

2. Here is a variant of a problem presented in Chapter 8 (p. 67). You have eight look-alike coins of which one is a heavier counterfeit. A balance scale is available and the counterfeit is to be located in two weighings. Present this problem to a friend; ask that person to think aloud while working out the solution.

Q_1: **What do you predict will be your friend's initial approach?**

A_1: People tend to divide the coins in half, 4 and 4 on each side of the scale, and then 2 and 2.

Q_2: **Why is this problem illustrating "set"?**

A_2: Because there are two sides to a balance scale and because 8 is an even number (i.e., readily divisible by 2) and, possibly, because it is known that 8 is a power of 2, most people will be set to divide the coins into two groups of 4 and 4. To solve the problem in two weighings, however, the coins must first be divided into *three* groups of 3, 3, and 2.

3. Can you connect the five dots at the right with three straight lines without lifting your pencil from the paper?

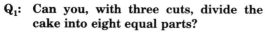
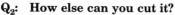

Q_1: **Why does this problem reflect einstellung?**

A_1: The usual set that people have is to connect the dots, to change line direction at each dot. You have to break away from that set, to extend the lines *beyond* the dots.

4. A researcher on problem solving gives you a candle, a few thumbtacks, and a box of safety matches.

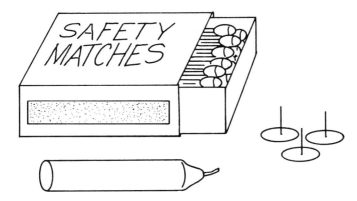

The experimenter points to a bulletin board against the wall and instructs you as follows: Using only these materials attach the candle to the board in such a way that you can safely light the candle; then light the candle. Describe how you would do this.

5. The figure at the right shows how, given three matches, you can make a triangle. With six matches, make four triangles all the same size as the one shown in the figure.

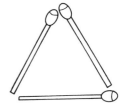

6. Twelve matchsticks are arranged into the pattern shown.

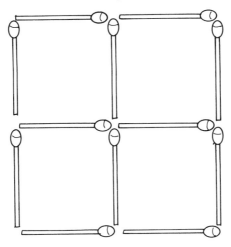

Remove two matches leaving exactly two squares.

7. You are called as a problem-solving expert to consult on a problem in a local factory. A small group of workers have the job of stuffing newspapers into barrels to keep the contents, pottery, from moving during shipment. The supervisor reports that the workers are constantly distracted by what they read in the papers as they are working. They stop to read the articles or they call news items to each other's attention. Sometimes everyone stops to read or even to argue about an article. A backlog frequently develops at this stage of production.

Q_1: **What can be done? Brainstorm a bit. How many different solutions can you come up with?**

A_1: Some obvious possibilities: Talk to the workers; give incentives for speeding up; pay, not hourly, but by the barrel stuffed; assign an additional supervisor to devote more time to this particular group.

Some more unusual suggestions: Hire illiterate people for this job, hire non-English speakers, keep the same employees but use foreign language newspapers (note how this solution evolves from the two preceding), blindfold the workers, employ blind workers. (This last alternative was suggested by the preceding and, because it fit with the company's policy to hire the handicapped, was favored by management. Notice how the crude and ridiculous notion of blindfolding workers led to a useful solution. Respect crude ideas!)

8. Suppose that you are a designer of new products for a firm that produces novelty items. Your problem is to find a couple of new items to propose at tomorrow's board meeting.

Q_1: **How many new uses can you think of for a pencil? Practice brainstorming. Write out your list before reading on.**

A_1: People tend to suggest a phone dialer, bookmark, weapon, pointer, dowel. Does your list contain more unusual alternatives? How about a measuring tool, swizzle stick, toothpick, pipe-bowl cleaner, fishing bob, nail cleaner, shoe horn.

Q_2: **Assume that you, as product designer, had generated the preceding list. Survey this list. What new products can you come up with?**

A_2: Here are a couple of suggestions:
(1) The pencil as a measuring instrument. Maybe an inch and/or millimeter scale can be printed along the length of the pencil. In one instrument, then, you would have both a ruler and a writer.
(2) A pencil as a swizzle stick or as a toothpick doesn't seem too hygienic. How about, however, a swizzle stick with a pointed end. It could be used in fruity drinks to spear the fruit as well as serving as a toothpick.

9. A young man's car developed a flat tire as he was driving along a deserted street. He pulled over to the curb and did all the usual things: removed the hub cap, unscrewed the lugs and rested them carefully in the hub cap, jacked up the car. As he was putting the spare tire onto the axle he accidentally kicked the hub cap. The lugs rolled out and all five of them fell down a nearby grate. Peering through the bars of the grate the man thought that he could see the lugs about six feet below in a shallow water puddle. He has a problem. How do you think he solved it?

10. A fellow was driving a truck whose top was 10 feet from the ground. He approached an overpass that carried a sign saying, "Low bridge. Vehicles 10 feet or higher must detour." Ignoring the sign he drove ahead. With a screech the roof of the truck jammed against the underside of the bridge. The truck got locked in, stuck. Full power applied to the engine couldn't budge the truck. What is the next step?

11. You are at a theater with your younger brother, reading the program, waiting for the play to begin. Your brother utters a cry of dismay and shows you that the right side-piece of his glasses has become separated, disconnected from the main frame. This is a new problem to you. You do not wear glasses and do not know much about them.

Q₁: What is the first thing to do?
A₁: Intimate engagement is called for. Study the point of junction of the side-piece and the frame. See how the two fit together. You observe the relationship shown in the following figure.

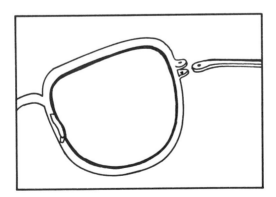

Q₂: How can you get additional information about how the two fit together?

A$_2$: Study the junction of the other, the left, side-piece of the glasses. This, being intact, will show you how the side-piece is normally attached to the frame. You observe that the holes in the frame and side-piece are lined up and a hinge is formed with a tiny screw. Obviously, the screw on the right side fell out.

You search for the screw on the seat and the nearby floor but do not find it. In the past you have seen people with a small safety pin at the corner of their glasses and you now understand why. However, you have no safety pin. You inquire of the people around you; they have none. The show will begin in about two minutes.

Q$_3$: **What else can you do?**
A$_3$: A little lateral thinking to overcome functional fixedness is needed now. You might remove a staple from the theater program and use it as a temporary hinge. Can you think of other solutions? Other methods for attaching two pieces together?

The language of riddles frequently induces an incorrect set. See how that works in these next problems.

12. You are wandering in the woods, lost, cold, and wet, when you come upon an abandoned cottage. Inside the cottage are three useful objects: a fireplace containing some dried branches, a stove that still has gas, and a kerosene lantern. You check your pockets and find that, fortunately, you have one dry match. Which do you light first?

13. It is noon, your lunch hour, but you cannot go out because there is a terrific hailstorm. Turning on your radio you hear the weathercaster predict that the hail will change to rain and that it will pour all day today. How can you determine whether the sun will be shining in 36 hours? Justify your answer.

14. Mary, Bill, and George are standing side by side in a straight line. Mary is to the right of Bill; George is to the right of Mary. Conclusion: Bill is to the left of George? No. Quite the contrary, Bill is to the right of George. How can that be?

15. A salesman traveled due west from city A to city B. The distance he traveled, that is, the distance from A to B, was *X* miles. He returned from B to A and found that he had traveled half the distance, *X*/2 miles. How can that be?

INTERPERSONAL PROBLEM SOLVING

11

THE PROBLEM-SOLVING STANCE

All the problems described in the preceding sections of this book had two common features. First, another person was not at the center of the problem. The problem solver confronted a physical situation (as in the repair of a toaster or the design of a roof) or a symbolic situation (as with mathematics problems or puzzles). The obstacles to solution were, correspondingly, physical or symbolic. All these problems were alike in this negative sense: They did *not* involve the needs, actions, or rights of another person. The second feature of all the preceding problems is that they engaged the mind in a pure way. We concentrated on strategies to be employed (e.g., use your eyes, look for special features) and on mental processes that interfered with solving the problem (einstellung). In short, the two characteristics of all the preceding problems are that they were *individual* and *intellectual*.

This chapter deals with problems that are different in both ways. First, another person is seen as having created the problem and/or is part of the obstacle toward a solution. That person must be considered or dealt with in solving the problem.

Here are two examples:

John A., a student living in the dorms, has for a neighbor a fellow who parties and plays his hi-fi set at full volume almost every night into the small hours of the morning. John, a serious student, is unable to sleep for the noise. He clearly has a problem, one caused by another person.

Mrs. K. is miserable because her husband, whom she otherwise likes and who is a wonderful father, flirts openly with other women at parties. Here again is a problem for one person produced by another.

Solving these problems will typically require dealing with that other person. This is one way in which these problems are different from virtually all the earlier ones discussed. We will refer to these new types of problems as interpersonal problems.

The second way in which interpersonal problems differ from the earlier ones is that they do not depend entirely upon intellectual skill although, as with any of the problems discussed earlier, good strategies and flexibility are important. However, a new component enters in, namely, one's own emotions. Specifically, we may see the necessary action to take but may be too intimidated, that is, fearful. (John may think of confronting his neighbor but is afraid of a scene.) Or we may be so carried away by our anger that we do no thinking at all. The anger runs our behavior. (Mrs. K. is frigidly cold toward her husband for two or three days after a party, saying nothing.) The anger may even make us behave badly, in ways that we later regret. Thus, in interpersonal problem solving, our own emotions are part of the obstacles to solution. These, too, must be considered in handling any such problem.

In this section, then, we will be dealing with problems between people. This, of course, covers a wide range from a problem between two individuals to large-scale political issues. We, however, will treat only the simplest of these problems, those involving two people. This, of course, is not a small or trivial class and is a type that you, the reader, will commonly encounter. Typically, such a problem will be within your control and will be your responsibility to solve. This is not to imply that interpersonal problems are always soluble or that you can't seek help. With any problem—for example, repairing a toaster— you may fail or you may seek help. I am saying simply that you will find yourself, from time to time, in a situation with another person that is obviously your problem.

Problems between two people may be divided into two categories. In the first, the problem solver is one of the two people in the situation. The examples given (John and his noisy neighbor, Mrs. K.) are of this sort. In the second, the two people involved are at some sort of impasse. Both are miserable, frustrated, and seemingly at a stalemate. They may call on an outside person to help with their dispute. In this case, problem solving involves a third party, a *mediator*. In recent years, both types of problems have received systematic treatment, along with sets of how-to-do-it rules, that is, prescriptive principles. The first category, in which the solver is within the situation, is treated under *social skills training* or *assertiveness training* (Alberti and Emmons, 1978; Lange and Jakubowski, 1976). The other, the three-person situation, is treated under *mediation training*. Since the principles for each are different in several details, we will review each one separately, beginning with the pure two-person problem.

Before we begin, however, I want to present *the* fundamental principle, common to both types of interpersonal problems. That principle is: *Take a problem-solving stance.* Train yourself; get into the habit of seeing interpersonal difficulties as problems to be solved, as engaging the mind. Most of the time, we do not do this—we react only emotionally. Someone frustrates us and we lash out. Our boss is unfair, and we privately grumble. With the problem-solving stance we bring our mind into it. We say "I don't like this situation. How can I change it?" Once you do that, all the principles you read about earlier can be brought to bear: intimate engagement (study the situation closely), lateral thinking, and so on. With the problem-solving stance, you try to get your emotions out of the way.

When, in a difficult interpersonal situation, you take a problem-solving stance, your behavior is marked by two features: You stress your own responsibility for solving the problem, and you look to the future. I said that one's attitude becomes "How can I change this situation?" The emphasis is on "I" and on "change," that is, on improving the future. Correspondingly, the signals of a failure to take the problem-solving stance are (1) harping only on what the other party should do (John says: "He should move out; he should cut out the parties." Mrs. K. says: "He should consider my feelings; he should stop flirting"), and (2) focusing on the past. Neighbors who have been feuding for a couple of years come into mediation insisting: "He should apologize" or "She owes me an explanation" or "He should be punished," always about incidents that happened weeks or even years ago. The problem-solving stance, by contrast, concentrates on what one can do oneself to improve the situation from this moment forward. John and Mrs. K. may be convinced that the best solution is for the other person's behavior to change. It is not enough, however, for them to insist on it repeatedly, indignantly, and, as in Mrs. K.'s case, only to themselves. If they want the other person's behavior to change, then their problem is to figure out how best to produce that change.

Let us consider the problem-solving stance concretely, with some examples. Here is one from a mediation session that I attended.

> The husband of a young wife would go out with one of his buddies "for an hour" and would come back two or three hours later. Resentment at being left alone builds up in the wife, and when the husband returns she starts scolding and yelling at him. This sequence, his staying out longer than he said and her yelling at him, would repeat itself two and three times a week.

In this situation, let's focus only on the wife and her problem: She is lonely and would like her husband to spend more time with her. She reacts only from her anger, not with her mind. She does not ask "What can I do to get him to spend more time with me?" That would be the start of the problem-solving stance. Instead, her anger directs her behavior: She yells. Suppose you were the wife in this situation. Do a little brainstorming. What kinds of alternative solutions can you come up with? (Remember, the rules in brainstorming are: Generate lots of solutions, and don't be critical.) A few of my suggestions are presented in the list that follows. How do yours compare?

*   *   *   *   *   *   *   *   *

Some solutions for the young wife:

1. At a time when you are both calm and feeling friendly, talk the problem over with him. Try to make him more aware of your needs, your loneliness, your affection for him.

2. Try to rekindle romance. With clothes and makeup, make yourself more attractive, even enticing so that he will want to stay home.
3. Join him with his friends occasionally.
4. Suggest that his friends visit half the time at your house.
5. Develop the kind of interests (sports, cards?) that draw him to his friends.
6. Here's an example of lateral thinking: Find new activities that will keep you busy on those evenings. Develop yourself and your own life.
7. By keeping busy in the right way (e.g., developing a skill, pursuing studies) gradually transform yourself into a more interesting person.

Have you thought of others?

*   *   *   *   *   *   *   *   *

Here is another example:

George is a neat person and easy to live with. His roommate, Bill, who is likeable and a good friend, has one disagreeable habit. He never hangs up his clothing or puts away his laundry. Pants are on the kitchen table, underwear is left on chairs, shoes clutter up the floor. For weeks George has grumbled in silence. (He has been too intimidated to do anything. Fear has run his behavior. This is definitely not the problem-solving stance.) This afternoon a date is coming to visit George. He has cleaned up the room, even hanging up his roommate's clothes. Bill comes in briefly, cheerfully congratulates George on his lucky date, promising to be out before she comes. Before leaving he changes his clothing and, you guessed it, leaves his old clothes discarded around the room. George blows up and starts yelling at him: You're always doing this; you're such a slob; you're so damned inconsiderate; and on; and on. From fear and irritation George has flip-flopped to anger.

This situation had been going on for weeks. At no time did George ask himself: What can I do to get him to hang up his clothes. That is, at no time did he take the problem-solving stance. He just grumbled in silence. For this problem, again, make a list of possible solutions. What might George have done during the several weeks instead of just silently grumbling? What might he have said or done on that fateful day?

*   *   *   *   *   *   *   *   *

Anger is generally a signal that you're *not* taking the problem-solving stance. You're in a nonsmoking car of a train. A fellow comes in and lights up a cigar. If your immediate impulse is to punch him in the nose, or verbally abuse him, or yell at him sarcastically ("Hey, wise-guy. Can't you read? It says NO SMOKING!") then you are not taking the problem-solving stance.

The question may occur to you "Why not punch the cigar-smoking fellow in the nose? Won't that solve the problem?" or "Maybe George *should* have yelled at his roommate. Isn't that what Bill deserved?" To deal with this kind of question, to understand why the problem-solving stance is better than thoughtlessly getting angry and blowing up, we have to look more deeply at what an interpersonal problem is.

Let's begin with an analogy. A man goes to a doctor complaining of a bad pain in his back. A thorough investigation fails to reveal any physical cause. The doctor prescribes a drug to eliminate the pain—and it works. The pain is gone. The only trouble is that the drug has a side effect. It makes the man perpetually sleepy so that he can't function. Has the man's problem (the pain in the back) been solved? Yes. In an ideal way? Absolutely not. The solution the man wanted was to live his life in the normal way but without the pain. Getting rid of the pain, however, was accompanied by unwanted side effects. Similarly, in interpersonal problem solving we want to solve the problem at its focus—get rid of the specific pain—without producing the side effects.

What kind of side effects are we referring to? Let's consider two of the examples just raised, the fellow lighting up in the No Smoking car and the roommate who leaves his clothes around. Presumably, the fellow who lights up is creating two problems: His smoke directly bothers us, and he is setting a bad example that others may follow. The problem is solved if he stops smoking. It is not solved if he is hurt physically or humiliated. Those are irrelevant side effects. It is certainly not solved if, in response to my insulting remark, he embarrasses me by blowing smoke in my face, or worse, punches me. Those are surely unwanted side effects. Thus, the ideal solution is one in which the problem is solved (he stops smoking) with no side effects. Consider George's problem with his roommate. George likes the guy. He doesn't particularly want another roommate. He doesn't want to live in a chronic state of complaints and hostility with his roommate. Those are unwanted side effects. George just wants the clothes hung up and, of course, a continuing friendly relation with his roommate.

We can characterize the problem-solving stance in its most general way as follows: In any given situation you and the other person have certain rights. Both of you have the right to be free of abuse and of harassment. Both have the right to satisfy important needs. Both have the rights defined by traditional understandings as well as by law. Occasionally, you will feel your rights are being violated. The problem-solving stance is one which seeks to correct that situation without particularly violating the other fellow's rights.

This is why fear and anger are undesirable extremes. When we are unable to act because we are intimidated then our rights are sacrificed. When we react with unthinking anger, then the other fellow's rights are violated. The problem-solving stance is between these two extremes. For this reason, I refer to it sometimes as the middle way. In taking the middle way we try to find some sensible balance among the differing claims.

Let us close this chapter by reviewing the initial example, that of the student, John, whose next-door dormitory neighbor plays loud music in the middle of the night. John, a serious and hard working student, wants to sleep at night but frequently cannot because of all the noise.

Suppose you were John. How would handle this problem? Do a little brainstorming. What solutions can you come up with? Before reading on, jot down your suggestions.

*   *   *   *   *   *   *   *   *

A common class of solution might include: Play your own hi-fi set loudly during the morning when your neighbor is sleeping. Throw a rock through his window with an unsigned note, saying, "Cut out the noise at night, or else!" Spray shaving cream under his door; be generally harassing until he moves.

These are all reprisal or vengeance solutions and stem primarily from anger. If all your solutions involve "getting back" at the guy, then anger is directing your actions; you are not taking the problem-solving stance.

Reprisals as a way of changing a person's behavior may sometimes be legitimate, but they shouldn't be all that you consider. In fact, because of the side effects they bring, they should come only after alternative solutions have been explored. How about these:

1. Talk to the fellow. Maybe he doesn't realize that anyone is being disturbed. In the high school he came from all his friends lived as he does. Talking to the fellow means, of course, that you will be complaining about or criticizing him to his face. How one criticizes effectively is gone into at some length in the next chapter.
2. If you're feeling generous, offer to buy him a set of inexpensive earphones. That way, you acknowledge his right to listen to loud music when he feels like it.
3. Try adjusting: You might try sleeping with earplugs. Or you might add insulation to the common wall of your two rooms—perhaps the college would pay for it.
4. Bring the law (in this case, the university rules) to bear: Check with your dorm counselor or the college housing office on whether the fellow isn't breaking established rules. Can they see to it that the rules are enforced?
5. Is it possible, and convenient, to change rooms?

There are, clearly, more alternatives than just vengeance solutions. I have organized the list according to how much trouble and possible side effects are involved. For any problem, I think, one can organize the alternatives along such a scale. By both these criteria, trouble and side effects, vengeance solutions usually belong at the end. If one takes the sensible route of starting at the top and going down, then vengeance solutions should be among the last considered, when nothing else works.

It is remarkable how often the simplest alternative, talking to the other person, is omitted. We saw that happen with the wife who yells and with George and his roommate. Did you think of it for this last problem? The wife we described at the outset, who was unhappy because her husband flirted at parties, never spoke to him about it. In fact, when a counselor suggested it, she became indignant. "Why should I? He should know better!" But this is the voice of anger (and, perhaps, intimidation). Her husband may not even be aware why she is so icy after a party. Talking, because of the low effort required and minimal side effects produced, should be an early solution to be explored. Its importance cannot be overemphasized. I once asked a friend whose wisdom I respect, what is her most important advice to young couples who are about to get married. "I tell them," she said, "always to try to talk with each other about their problems." Simple talking as a way of solving a problem is so valuable that the next chapter is devoted entirely to it.

In summary, then, the fundamental principle of interpersonal problem solving is to take a problem solving-stance. This entails (1) getting your emotions out of the way; (2) focusing on the future, that is, on the changes you want from here on out; and (3) taking responsibility for producing those changes. Once you take such a stance, a little thought will suggest a variety of possibilities, from talking to the other person, to finding compromises, to adapting, to seeking assistance, to reprisals. These alternatives generally can be ordered in terms of how little effort and how few unwanted side effects they are likely to produce. Topping such a scale, for almost every problem, would be talking to the other person.

INTERPERSONAL PROBLEM SOLVING

12

RIGHT SPEECH:

How to Give

Criticism

We said that we are dealing here with problems that arise between two people. Most of the time, the problem takes the form that, from your point of view, the other person is doing something wrong, is creating the problem for you. Since, as we just discussed, talking to the other person is a useful first step, most of the time the solution requires criticizing the other person. Our concern in this chapter may be expressed as: How can we criticize so that we will be most effective, that is, so that the problem is solved with minimal side effects? In talking to the other person, our aim is to win his or her cooperation in bringing about the solution. How can we best evoke a cooperative attitude from the other person? Several principles have emerged and are routinely taught for dealing with such problems. In this chapter we will review four of them: Presenting yourself, I-talk, the Mary Poppins rule, and the comic parry. Let us consider each in turn.

PRESENTING YOURSELF

This concerns not what you do, but rather how you do it. The basic recommendations are: 1. Maintain good eye contact, that is, look at the person in an informal conversation style; 2. use a good voice, that is, speak to be understood using an audible but not loud voice. This is the middle way in contrast the two extremes. An overly timid approach involves looking away—fearing to face the other person and mumbling or speaking too softly. An overly angry approach is overbearing—you frown and stare at the other person as though he or she were a troublesome child; you raise your voice and scold. In the middle way, you appear confident, ready to stand up for your rights, without appearing to show illwill toward the other fellow. Remember, we're looking for the most effective way to solve the problem with the minimum of side effects. Begin by making the situation into as human an interaction as possible. The key words are eye contact and good voice.

I-TALK

Our focus is on presenting criticism so that it will be effective. It has been noted by several authors that a blunt statement of the criticism, "telling it like it is" (e.g., George telling his roommate "You're such a slob!"; Mrs. K. says to her flirtatious husband "You have some nerve") is not apt to be effective. The reason is that blunt criticism has the sound of an attack; the person then gets his guard up, becomes defensive and resentful. The likely result is that he attacks back or simply defends himself. The solving of the problem gets lost in the process. How, then, does one effectively express the criticism, one's displeasure? By describing it. What you want to convey is just that, your displeasure, your unhappiness about the situation. Thus, George can say "I don't know why, Bill, but it annoys me to see clothing all over the place. Here we both work hard to keep the rooms clean yet it still looks like a mess. The reason is simple. There are clothes everyplace you look. It's embarrassing when friends come over. Don't you think it would help if we each directly hung our things up?"

Notice certain features in this example of how to present criticism:

1. George never insults Bill. Instead of "You this" and "You that" he says "it annoys me." He conveys his unhappiness by describing it rather than by condemning the other person. The emphasis shifts from "You're a slob" to "I'm unhappy; I have a problem." This is the essence of I-talk.
2. Also, he describes the situation objectively, as it might be seen by an outside observer: "The place looks like a mess." "There are clothes everyplace you look." "It's embarrassing." Again, no accusations are made. You want the other person to see the problem the way that you do and, therefore, to be more willing to cooperate in the solution.
3. In addition to conveying his unhappiness, he proposes a reasonable solution: "Don't you think it would help if we each directly hung our things up?"
4. While we cannot show in this book the tone of voice or how eye contact is made, we do see another kind of attempt to humanize the situation: George begins by using Bill's name. Among friends this is a natural supplement to eye contact and good voice.

For another example of I-talk, consider the wife whose husband stayed out evenings and whose only response was to yell at him. I suggested that she might, in a calm hour, talk to him. The presentation of her feelings in I-talk might go something like this: "I'm alone all day, John, and then I'm left alone in the evening. It's too much. I get lonely. I'd love it if we could spend more time together." Note not only the I-talk but the use of the name, the objective description ("It's too much"), and the positive suggestion. This I-talk style is apt to be more effective than "You're always leaving me. You're so inconsiderate. All you think about is yourself." The first approach invites John's cooperation in solving the wife's problem. The second approach forces John to defend himself. We would not be surprised with the second approach if John started insisting on all the things he did for this marriage and on all the ways the wife thinks only of herself. The original problem will have gotten lost.

THE MARY POPPINS RULE

This takes its name from a theme in the film *Mary Poppins* that was repeated again and again, and was even sung about: *A spoonful of sugar helps the medicine go down.* We have suggested that blunt criticism, no matter how well it expresses your righteous indignation, is not an effective way to get the other person's cooperation. More likely, it makes him or her defensive and hostile. When you find yourself facing a problem caused by another person, your goal is to get the other person to change his or her behavior or, at least, to be cooperative in finding a solution. In other words, you don't just want to insist indignantly that you are right; you want to be effective. In general, then, we want to find ways to stand up for our rights, to communicate our displeasure, but to soften the criticism so that it will be better received. We have already seen two ways of speaking that have precisely this "softening" function: conversational style and I-talk. The Mary Poppins rule adds other methods.

Ever since we were small children we have been taught: When you want something, ask for it politely. Preface requests with "Please," or "Would you mind . . .," or "May I . . .". Why should we do that? Why is "May I please have that" better than "Give me that"? Both state the same message: You have something and I want it. Why is the person more likely to cooperate with the first form than with the second? I was in a movie theater recently. Although the film hadn't started, the theater was crowded. A fellow, Mr. A, was sitting in front of me with an empty seat on either side of himself. Another man, Mr. B, came walking down the aisle with his wife and said as he passed me, "there are two seats." He then went to Mr. A and said "Hey. Move over. We want to sit together." What do you think happened? Mr. A visibly stiffened and said "I'm not moving." Why? Why did Mr. A react like that? Let's consider why he might not have felt like cooperating.

In any interpersonal problem situation, both people have—or feel that they have—certain traditional rights. Here, Mr. A may sit in an empty seat of his choosing; Mr. B may sit with his wife. Consider some of the other examples in terms of rights. The husband, after working hard all day and earning a good wage, feels he has the right to relax in whatever way he pleases; the wife, after being alone all day, feels she has the right to some companionship. George does his share of work around the room and feels he has the right to a neat room; Bill feels he has the right to put his own clothing wherever he likes. An important step in getting another person to change is to see that offending person's rights, *and to acknowledge that he or she has those rights.* When you are polite, you are making precisely that acknowledgment.

What is the alternative to politeness? It is a command. ("Move over.") A command, however, is the language of a master to a slave. It says, in effect, "You have no rights. You must do as I say." A polite mode of expression, on the other hand, says "You do have some rights, but I'm asking you to forgo these in part and to cooperate." Thus, if Mr. B. had said "Would you mind moving over?" he would be acknowledging that Mr. A had some rights in the situation. We can safely presume that that would have been more effective, that Mr. A would have been more likely to move.

As I have noted, the Mary Poppins rule is: A spoonful of sugar helps the medicine go down. The sense of that is: To make your criticism most effective, most likely to be taken seriously, make it more palatable. This, of course, is the function of those behaviors already considered: conversational style, I-talk, and polite language. The direct form of the Mary Poppins rule, however, is a compliment. Try to preface the criticism with an honest, appropriate positive comment. Thus George, who in fact likes Bill, could start a discussion of the clothing problem with the following: "You know, Bill, I really like you and I'm happy that we're roommates. I've got to tell you, though, I'm bugged by one thing. We both work hard, the place is always a mess, . . ."

I am not talking here about empty flattery. The positive expression should be appropriate to the relationship and to the situation. Frequently, however, the compliment, the statement of affection, is completely true but in the heat of indignation is overlooked. Consider again the wife who yells at her husband because he spends several evenings away from her. She surely likes being with him. Otherwise, what is all the fuss about? Along with the I-talk just described, she might include this sentiment: "Part of my problem, John, is that I like you and I like being with you. I miss you when we're apart. Don't you think we might . . . ?"

In Buddhist philosophy there is a basic commandment, *use right speech*, where right speech has been characterized (Rahula, 1974) as speech that avoids creating antagonisms and, rather, has the effect of reducing antagonisms. I-talk, politeness, and complimentary, even affectionate, expressions are examples of right speech in the service of the problem-solving stance.

THE COMIC PARRY (OR KEEP IT LIGHT)

This final principle deals with the use of humor and wit in problem situations. It is different from the others because the problems are typically less serious than the ones so far considered. For the most part, the problem arises suddenly and does not usually have profound consequences. Nevertheless, humor can be useful in eliminating occasional obstacles between people. A favorite example involved my daughter.

> My wife and I took my daughter and her then boyfriend out to a restaurant to celebrate some occasion or other. My daughter started out by being a bit edgy—she criticized the restaurant, she complained about the menu, then remarked that the soup wasn't hot enough. Her boyfriend turned to her and, with a sharper tone than he probably intended, said, "you're awfully picky." I thought to myself, "Oh, oh, the evening is ruined. She's going to get angry; they won't talk to each other for an hour; it will be tense; etc." However, my daughter laughed and responded, "No I'm not. I go out with you, don't I?"

Thus, instead of becoming angry or moody, she found a way to keep it light. We all saw the humor in the remark. The boyfriend, shaking his head, said, "Boy! I asked for that one"—he too kept it light. Instead of a glum situation they created a jovial, cheerful atmosphere.

This example is a prototype of the situation in which the comic parry is effective. One person criticizes, offends, or even insults another. The target of the unpleasantness responds, but with wit, in a light-hearted way. Here is another example:

> The chairperson of a large biology department gave her secretary, who was young and relatively new in the position, a set of documents. She informed her that the faculty would be coming by to read these and that it would be better if the papers did not circulate. The faculty had been asked to read them in the secretary's office. One of the senior faculty came in later and requested the documents. He announced that he would be taking them to read in his office. The secretary resisted a bit and dutifully reminded him of the policy. The professor, starting to become impatient, insisted on taking them. The following exchange then took place:
> Secretary: "Will you be bringing them back?"
> Professor: (Clearly irritated, almost sneering) "No. I am going to throw them out."
> Secretary: (Brightly) "Good! You'll save us all a lot of work."

The professor, by his tone and facial expression said that the secretary's question was stupid. The secretary, instead of crumbling at the remark and brooding afterward, kept it light. By bantering she deflected the insult.

I think that I first noticed wit as a method for countering a putdown in the following anecdote that I read as a boy.

The minister was being shaved by the town barber, who had been partying the night before. He still smelled of whiskey, and was a bit unsteady from being hung over. In the course of the shave he nicked the minister's skin a couple of times. After the third time the minister remarked, "Ah, my son, it is terrible to get drunk." To which the barber responded, "Yes, it makes the skin very tender."

I'm sure that we all agree that the light-hearted reply is an effective way to deal with the person who would make us defensive. The difficulty is that wit is a rare gift. If someone is arrogant or insulting or generally offensive, we would love to have a witty comeback, but we rarely can think of the right thing to say. If wit is such a rare gift, what good is it to speak of the comic parry as a general principle of interpersonal problem solving? The light-hearted response, however, doesn't depend entirely upon brilliant improvised cleverness. In some cases, there are stylized responses that you can make. These tend to be keyed to specific situations. Here are a few of these situations along with an appropriate response.

Sarcasm.   A friend of mine has a standard response when someone speaks to him sarcastically. (Assume that I just got huffy and said "Yeah, you're smart. Everyone knows you're the smartest guy in town.") "Marvin," he would say, "you're being sour-castic." That word, being a pun, introduces an element of humor into a potentially antagonistic situation. Also it subtly turns back the offense: The speaker is the one who is being "sour." Notice that this response doesn't call for creative genius. Whenever you recognize that a friend is being sarcastic, the response can be called up.

Arrogance.   Do you remember that when we were children we used to return an insult by putting our thumb to our nose and waggling our fingers at the person? An acquaintance of mine, a college professor no less, uses a version of this when a friend is being arrogant. Thus, in a discussion the friend may say "now you don't know enough about politics to realize how lobbies operate, but I've studied political science and I can tell you . . ." The professor will scratch his nose with his thumb, waggle his fingers, and say with a grin "Excuse me but my nose itches." The humor typically gets across to the friend and tones him down with fewer side effects than getting angry or telling him bluntly that he is being arrogant.

Indignation over lack of trust.   Another friend has a standard response when, in money matters, the other person is too casual. He had loaned an acquaintance some money and had asked for a written receipt, an I.O.U. The recipient became indignant, saying "What's the matter. Don't you trust me?" My friend replied, "Listen, I trust my mother. But when we play cards I cut the deck."

The wisecrack. A joke that I know is the source of another response that we use in my family.

> The joke goes: The elephant was thirsty, went down to the river, and put his trunk in the water to drink. Seeing him drinking, the crocodile thought that he would have some fun. He swam under the water until he was just below the elephant's trunk, opened his jaws, and snapped them shut on the trunk. The elephant looked at the crocodile and said "veddy fuddy."

A friend says to my son "Boy, that's some haircut. Did you pay the barber or are you suing him for damages?" My son is apt to reply "veddy fuddy."

These then are a few stylized responses to standard kinds of offensive remarks. With a little experience and thought, you might add others to this list. Notice a couple of details about these responses. They don't demand great cleverness. They simply require that you learn to recognize these characteristic situations (sarcasm, arrogance, the issue of trust, wisecracks). The response will soon become fairly routine. Like all of wit, these responses all have a common quality, light-heartedness. Because you have a humorous response at hand you don't take the offense so seriously. When we were kids we used to have a whole collection of responses to challenges and insults ("Oh yeah? So's your old man." "Yer mudder wears combat boots." "You want to fight? . . . Join the army.") They had a quality of bantering; they kept things light. That's the effect we want to achieve.

A potential reaction to this chapter is "I hear your message; I like it and I think you're right. But in a tense situation I get tongue-tied and can't say the right words, or I get so angry that I'm shouting before I think about it." Thus, learning to take the problem-solving stance has a special difficulty. This learning is overwhelmed and suppressed by deeply ingrained emotional habits. We have this old strong habit of reacting angrily.

The only answer to that is: Commit yourself to change. Start working on changing those habits. It will be slow, perhaps a matter of years. There will be backsliding. Nevertheless, one can change. An emotional response is primarily a habit and, as such, is subject to change (for an excellent analysis of anger as a habit, see Tavris, 1982). For example, there are commonplace techniques for cooling anger:

breathing deeply, counting to ten, seeing the situation through the other person's eyes. Start developing the habit of employing these techniques when you find yourself becoming angry.

Perhaps the greatest ally in dealing with anger is time. Anger creates a kind of einstellung; it narrows our choice of solutions to those where we lash out at the other person. With the passage of time, anger diminishes, and we become free then to consider more alternatives. Here is a dramatization of an incident that came to my attention.

The owner of a small chain of diners had just opened a new restaurant and had hired four waitresses, two full-time and two part-time. The owner worked in this particular branch on Mondays with Phyllis, one of the part-time waitresses. The other three were off that day. He had given the four women a firm command: Because their income depended so much on tips, they were to take turns waiting on customers. Fairness in this matter was important to good morale. One Monday, when Phyllis was alone with the owner, she complained to him about Marge, one of the full-time waitresses. Marge, she said, was "jumping the line," taking the tables when it was her, Phyllis's, turn. Marge had insisted that it was her right as a full-time worker.

As the owner puts it: "I was furious. I had seen in the other places the troubles this caused. If Marge had been there I would have fired her on the spot." He then added, "As luck has it, she wasn't there. I didn't see her until two days later. By then I had cooled off and was thinking that maybe Marge had misunderstood me or that there was some mistake. When I finally saw her I took her aside, told her what Phyllis had said and asked what was going on?"

"'Me jump the line?' answered Marge. 'That's a laugh. It's Phyllis. I had to talk to her about it a couple of times. Check with the others.'"

"I checked with the others. They backed up Marge. Phyllis, they insisted, was pushy and took tables when it wasn't her turn. Marge was right to talk to her. Even the chef said that Phyllis was a complainer. They turned my head completely around. Even though I hadn't been unpleasant with Marge I still apologized to her."

The critical feature in this story is the passage of two days. At first the angry owner considered only a single alternative: fire, scold, or otherwise punish Marge. Two days later he could approach the problem more sensibly: "What is going on?"

Count to ten—and then count to one hundred. Try not to handle a problem in a state of anger or indignation. Wait a bit. It will permit you to expand the range of possible actions.

A second method for dealing with the emotional obstacles is consistent with some of the ideas of the earlier chapters. The point of view that we are adopting here is that anger is a habitual response to situations. It is strongly ingrained, to be sure, but, like any habit, it can be changed. An important procedure for changing a habitual response is to replace it with a new response and to practice that new response. We saw in Chapter 5 (p. 37) that when we are not able to carry out the new behavior actively, in the situation itself, then we can do so in imagination. We saw, for example, that we are more likely to remember to buy eggs on the way home from work if we actively picture ourselves driving home from work and pulling over to park by the grocery. We suggested rehearsing this scenario in imagination a few times during the day.

This rehearsal is similarly effective with an interpersonal problem situation, although more than simple remembering is involved.

A happily married husband who works hard, both at his job and around the house, has a small problem. His wife, who is currently between jobs, and who is still asleep in the morning when he leaves for work, has started neglecting to make the bed. The husband knows that as life's problems go this one is trivial, but he hates going to sleep every night in a rumpled bed. That problem, small as it is, is gnawing at him. His impulse is to shout at his wife: "All you do is sit around all day [He knows this is not true]. Can't you make the goddam bed?" You can imagine all the side effects—the tears, fighting, silences, recriminations—that that will produce. Instead, he decides to replace that little fantasy of lashing out with another. He will put up with the unmade bed for another day or two until he can find a quiet moment alone with his wife. Then the approach will be "Honey, there's something I'd like to talk about. Something has been bothering me, lately. I know it is a small thing, but . . ."

The husband's instincts are good. Notice the shift from "you" to "I." Notice the affectionate opening. What more can be done? *The husband rehearses the new scenario.* On the train home from work he goes over it a few times in his mind. Practicing being warm and conversational makes it less likely that, in the situation itself, he will become angry or intimidated. The rehearsal replaces the anger-attack impulse with a conversational-request fantasy. Practicing the behavior in imagination will make it more available in the real situation.

Success breeds success. Each time you substitute the problem-solving stance for an uncontrolled emotional outburst, it will make it easier to take that stance in future situations. Gradually, the new habits will replace the old. This change from automatic emotional reaction to a more thoughtful, objective style will improve your skills in social problem solving. You gradually will acquire the reputation for tact and diplomacy and will find a greater harmony coming into your life.

INTERPERSONAL PROBLEM SOLVING

13

SOLVING OTHER PEOPLE'S PROBLEMS:

Let It Happen

In this chapter we will continue to consider interpersonal problems, problems that arise between two people. However, there is a change. Previously, we considered situations in which you might be one of the two people. Now you are an outsider. The only reason that the problem exists as a problem for you is that the two people involved have turned to you for assistance. To use the current popular term, you are asked to be a mediator, to mediate their dispute.[6]

Mediation has arisen recently as a formal method for resolving conflicts. Initially, it was employed to deal with issues between groups, such as between management and labor union representatives. More recently, the law courts have sponsored mediation for troubles between individuals, as an alternative to a trial. The typical situation involves two ordinary citizens, neither of whom has any criminal record, who get into some sort of dispute. For example, two neighbors might have a long-standing argument because one of them plays his music too loud and too late at night. The other gets particularly furious on one of these occasions, goes out, and throws a brick through the neighbor's window. Thereupon, this neighbor, the music player, calls the police. When the charges reach the district attorney's office, he has a decision to make. Clearly no criminals are involved. Also, no serious crime was committed. Furthermore, the crime that did take place was part of a history involving provocation. For such a case, the district attorney may very well refer it to mediation rather than have to go to the courts. If he does, the two parties would then appear before a mediator, possibly a professional but more typically a carefully selected and well-trained volunteer. The mediator would help the two parties resolve not only the issue over the broken window and how much is to be paid, but also the more chronic issues that continually troubled them.

Of course, mediation may occur without the instigation by the law courts. Today, the services of professional mediators are available to help arrange equitable divorce settlements; mediation is occasionally used in marriage counseling for specific problems. Furthermore, mediation can take place without professionals or formal structure. For example, married friends may come to you as an outside objective viewer for assistance in connection with a dispute. Or you may find yourself in the middle of a running argument between two people with whom you are sharing an apartment. The essential ingredients for mediation are two people (or two small groups of people—sometimes two feuding families come in for mediation)with some sort of problem between them and an outsider who can view the problem situation without self-interest, that is, who has no reason for taking sides.

---

[6]I want to thank Ernie Odom, director of the Community Mediation Center of Suffolk County, N.Y., for first acquainting me with the principles of mediation.

Because mediation is becoming so prevalent and because mediators require training, systematic principles have been distilled that have become the basis for training and practice. Since these are, essentially, prescriptive principles of problem solving, it is appropriate that we consider them here. Before doing so, however, let's look at the procedures of a typical mediation session.

Mediation needs some space. As you will see in a moment, it is a good idea to have a couple of rooms available. A typical session begins with the two parties and the mediator coming together in one of the rooms. At the outset, certain ground rules are announced: While one person is speaking the other is not to interrupt; both are to stay seated (a precaution against an outburst of violence); insults are to be avoided. The speakers are encouraged to stay close to the facts of the case, that is, to the history of events that brought them to the present problem. Furthermore, assurances are given about confidentiality—the disputants must have confidence that the mediator will not gossip.

After the mediator has described these ground rules, the procedure proper begins. Each person, usually starting with the one that brought the complaint, presents his or her side of the story. After each party has spoken and has had a chance to respond to statements that the other has made, the mediator sees each one privately, while the other waits in the second room. After seeing each one this way, the mediator may see them each again alone or may again have them come together. The ultimate resolution is some sort of explicit agreement. In formal mediation this is made in writing and has the status of a contract. In informal mediation, where, say, friends have come to you for assistance,a contract is not essential. It helps, however, to have agreements stated explicitly about what each individual will and will not do in the future. Even in such cases, where writing a contract seems artificial, it is wise for the mediator to make a note of the agreements and to file it away, just in case the friends later have differences over what they agreed to.

These, then, are the mediation procedures. What are the principles? We will describe here four. The first two we have already seen; they are relevant to any interpersonal problem. The others are more specific to the mediation procedure.

TAKE THE PROBLEM-SOLVING STANCE

Both parties will come in, each filled with righteous indignation, angry at the other one, convinced the other is totally in the wrong. The attitude that the mediator by his manner must communicate is: There is a problem here; how can we best solve it? By taking the problem-solving stance, the mediator becomes a model for the disputants, show-ing another way to approach life's difficulties.

Taking the problem-solving stance as a mediator has special implications. Two qualities must be part of this attitude. The first is: *Don't judge.* The mediator's function is *not* to decide right and wrong, is *not* to assign blame. He is there only to help the parties solve their problem. Typically, this attitude is described explicitly before the mediation actually begins. The statement is made to the participants that they are not there to be judged. They are there, rather, to try to solve whatever the problem is.

The second quality is: *Avoid bias.* The mediator must be sensitive to his or her own inner reactions and must avoid taking sides. If you find yourself facing a marital argument where you "hate him; love her", you'll probably do more harm than good. Beware of thoughts like "She's a liar" or "He's such a slob."

EYE CONTACT AND GOOD VOICE

We said in the preceding chapter that when you're in an interpersonal problem, try to maintain a warm, human relationship by presenting yourself properly. This certainly applies in mediation. Use a comfort-able conversational style, including eye contact appropriately with each of the parties, and a good voice. This helps to transmit a sense of goodwill and concern for both parties. This, in turn, helps communi-cate the problem-solving stance. An atmosphere in which the medi-ator's manner avoids tension will facilitate a more reasonable, problem-solving attitude by the disputants.

LET IT HAPPEN

The cardinal rule of mediation is: The agreements most likely to endure are those proposed and negotiated by the parties themselves. A solution imposed by the mediator is more likely to be resisted. In good mediation the parties do most of the talking. The mediator simply guides the process. The two main questions that form the guidelines are: (in the opening phase) What is your side of the story? and (in a later phase) How would you like to see this situation resolved? In connection with this second question, the mediator tries to shift the focus that the people have from the past on to the future. As I men-tioned earlier, people will insist on punishment, justice, an apology, an explanation, all for past incidents. They are hoping for some recogni-tion by the mediator that they were in the right and the other party was wrong. Typically, both people feel this way. The real problem, however, is that the parties have to continue living in the same physical arrangements, for example, as neighbors. How shall they behave with each other from this time forth?

In discussing each person's suggested solutions, the mediator may, if necessary, encourage the parties to be realistic and, again if necessary, remind each one that the other has some rights. Thus, one neighbor may say of another, "Let him move away. Everything was fine until he came." The mediator could respond with something like "That would certainly solve the problem. But it's unlikely that he'll move, and he has the right, of course, to stay where he is. Let's assume that he won't be moving. What then, do you think would solve the problem?" The mediator should not be afraid of silences. He or she lets the people work out their own solutions. The word that best describes a successful mediator is "nondirective." Such a mediator facilitates the solutions; helps the parties develop realistic solutions. But he or she doesn't "direct," doesn't impose the solutions.

THE "WHAT IF" PRINCIPLE

Suppose in characterizing their aims, the parties are at a stalemate. One neighbor says "I want him to stop playing that awful music"; the other says "We're not here because of my music. We're here because he threw a stone through my window. I want him to pay for it." And neither one seems to budge. This is one point at which the mediator stops being nondirective and takes an active role. Even now, however, a solution is not simply announced, but is, rather, suggested in a tentative way. The mediator's aim is not to impose what he or she thinks is a perfect solution but to get some ideas onto the table that the parties can explore. The ultimate resolution of the problem, remember, must come from them. This tentative way of making a suggestion is called the "What if" statement. Thus, the mediator might say "What if we tried to work out some compromise" and might then offer a suggestion "What if you (Mr. A) paid for the window without making Mr. B go to court, and you (Mr. B) restricted the time that you played your music. Could we work something out along those lines?"

Here is where lateral thinking can play a part. The mediator, being detached from the problem, is in a position to suggest some creative possibilities. Consider this example. A man in his thirties was having a running feud with a twelve-year-old boy who lived about a block from the man's house. The man insisted that, over a period of months, the boy had engaged in a series of petty vandalisms against his property. The boy had scratched his car, had knocked over his mailbox, his garbage, and so forth. The boy admitted only to scratching the car—he said the man nearly ran him down "on purpose" so he had picked up a stone and threw it at the car. Afterward, at his parents' insistence, he telephoned the man and apologized (the man agreed that that had happened). The man was angry with him over the phone and hung up. The boy's parents claimed that the man was known as a troublemaker in the neighborhood and that he was currently involved in a lawsuit with one of his neighbors.

What is lateral thinking in this situation? The parties, themselves, are generally looking for vengeance or "justice" (by which they mean that the other party should be punished) or for getting the other person out of their lives. Hostile thoughts are, typically, all that occur to them. Lateral thinking could entail doing something positive. For example, in this case, when the mediator was alone with the man, he said (he had learned that the man liked baseball): "What about trying to make a friend of the boy? Win him over. What if you took him to a ballgame?" In general, a search for appropriate positive alternatives is one "lateral" way to come at these situations. Again, of course, the mediator must not push too hard. He only makes the suggestion and hopes that, sooner or later, it takes hold.

These, then, are the principles of mediation. They do not seem like much, especially where the mediator just "lets it happen." Nevertheless, the data indicate that mediation has been phenomenally successful. Of the cases referred to mediation in my own community, over 80 percent are resolved and never again appear in the courts. If the mediator is so generally nondirective, why is mediation so successful?

There are three reasons for this success. First, it gives people a chance to "vent," or express, their anger, to release some of their frustrations. They present their arguments not only in the presence of the other party but in the presence also of a sympathetic listener, the mediator. Frequently, much of the hostility dissipates after the opening joint session. The people become more receptive to some sort of negotiation.

The second reason is the other side of the coin. The parties hear, perhaps for the first time, their adversary's complaints. They can hear them as human beings with their own needs and rights. Furthermore, the mediator is listening respectfully to that other point of view. Mediation, thus, provides the opportunity to see and hear the other party, that they are less evil or ridiculous than they were previously thought to be.

The third and, in my opinion, the major reason for the success of mediation is the problem-solving stance. Up until this point, the parties have known only frustration and anger. I mentioned in the previous chapter the wife who responds to her husband's neglect by yelling at him. In this chapter we saw the fellow who, in frustration, throws a brick through his neighbor's window. These people are now in a situation where, perhaps for the first time, they must talk things over. In a sense, the situation requires that they look for a solution, that they take the problem-solving stance. The mediator helps create this atmosphere by his or her own attitude. Frequently, mediation is an education for people. In the course of it they learn firsthand that you can take a less emotional, more intelligent attitude toward even the most intense personal problems. The spirit of mediation is: Reasonable people try to solve their problems. Even though that statement is never made to the participants, the sense of it is probably picked up by them and may well be responsible for the long-range benefits.

Whatever the reasons, the data suggest that the principles work. If you are a caring person, one who would like to improve some of the skills for helping others, you would do well to review closely these principles and to employ these procedures.

EXERCISES FOR INTERPERSONAL PROBLEM SOLVING

(*Note*: With interpersonal problems, there is rarely a single right answer. Any suggested solution must be evaluated by its potential effectiveness and its side effects. Compare and evaluate your own answers against those given here.)

1. A young woman, a school teacher, married a salesman in September. During the school year they both arose at the same time each weekday morning to go off to their respective jobs. When summer came, however, the woman was able to sleep later, although her husband continued to rise for work at the usual early hour. To the wife's unhappiness, the husband was as noisy as ever in the morning. He walked heavily, he sang while he shaved, he turned on the TV in the next-door room of their small apartment. The wife would lie in bed irritated every morning. Her impulse was to go to him and scold "You're so inconsiderate. Here I am trying to sleep and you're making the noise of an elephant! Didn't your folks ever teach you to be quiet when people are sleeping?" So far she had been able to suppress her anger and had not said these things. She felt, however, that she would explode any morning. She was afraid of a scene and an argument, but one of these mornings . . .

Q_1: Notice the combination of fear and anger that the teacher is experiencing. What is the middle way?

A_1: She might talk to her husband at a neutral time, say, in the evening, when she is not overwhelmed by the emotions.

Q_2: What is "right speech" here?

A_2: Her stance should be that "I have a problem," not that "You're inconsiderate." I-talk, good voice, comfortable terms of endearment could all be used.

Q_3: How might she handle her anger?

A_3: Waiting until a neutral time is one step. She might also practice in imagination the talk they will have: how she will initiate the conversation using I-talk, how she will handle it if he becomes defensive, and so on.

2. Tim and Tom are doing their college algebra homework together. Tim has a tendency to barge ahead working on a problem without reading it carefully. As a result he frequently starts a problem incorrectly. After one particularly bad blunder, Tom says, "You know, it's amazing. The brightest students have to read a problem carefully, maybe two or three times, then they have to think about it before putting a pencil to paper. Not you. You just have to glance at the problem; you don't have to think

about it. You're able to start right in. It must be wonderful to have this lightning mind where other people have to think and plod. Teach me how you do it. It would save me a lot of time. . . ." (Tom continues in this fashion).

Q_1: **Tim, who was first feeling foolish for his blunder, is now feeling putdown. Any suggestions for Tim?**

A_1: He might point out that Tom is being sour-castic (he also might indicate that the point about slowing down is well taken. Tom's message, after all, is good; it is the sarcasm that is bad).

3. A husband and wife, married about five years and parents of two children, appear at a mediation center to discuss a crisis. During the last two or three months, the wife has grown distant from the husband. At the mediation session she insists repeatedly that she wants a divorce. The husband does not want the divorce. He says that they had a good marriage up until the last few months and that there are the children to think of. He suggests that the wife is in some temporary "state." Although the mediator does not say it, her sense also is that the wife's attitude is short term, that definitive action like a divorce may be regretted later.

Q_1: **The couple is at a stalemate, with the wife insisting on a divorce and the husband refusing. It is time for a *what if* statement. If you were the mediator, what would you suggest?**

A_1: The mediator, talking to each of the parties privately, suggested a trial separation. "What if you tried living your own lives separately for a few months?"

The wife grudgingly agreed but insisted on no less than a six-month period. Also, she would stay home (they had earlier revealed that they owned a large house) with the children, and he would move out. The husband, when the *what if* statement was made to him, said that he could not do it: his business was off for the last couple of years so that they couldn't afford two residences.

Q_2: **A new stalemate. You wait to see if either of the two people have any suggestions, but they do not. What now?**

A_2: The mediator made the suggestion of an in-house separation. Could the couple organize things so that, with both residing in the house, they could each live their own lives, avoiding the other? They might restrict contact to neutral matters like problems concerning the children and business transactions. The husband and wife both reacted favorably to this suggestion and spent the rest of the session planning details of the arrangement. At a one-month follow-up they indicated that the plan was working. After four months, family life had returned to normal.

4. You share an apartment with three other students. The apartment has one telephone. One of the students has an overactive social life and monopolizes the phone. He makes and receives many calls; a single call might last for an hour. Your friends and family have complained that your line is always busy.

Q₁: **Brainstorm a bit. What suggestions can you come up with for handling the phone situation?**

A₁: Here are a few possibilities (what is your list like?):

1. Talk to the person (this may work best if all three of the unhappy residents appear together and present a united front).

2. Suggest a voluntary limit of the duration of any one call (e.g., 5 minutes—the amount should be negotiable).

3. Establish "prime time" hours, such as 7–10 P.M. during which the duration is limited.

4. Keep a record pad by the phone. Have people record the time speaking. Pay shares of the phone bill accordingly.

5. Try to persuade the fellow to get his own phone.

5. A young woman, Judy, has her third date with Jack. She likes Jack and has enjoyed her previous times with him. He has, however, been late for each of these dates. Now, again, it is 20 minutes after the appointed time when he is first seen approaching. Judy had said nothing after the first two meetings, although she felt bothered. This time it is particularly irritating because she had to wait for him in the street, in front of a store where they had arranged to meet. She makes up her mind to speak to him.

Q₁: **What should be the purpose of her criticism?**

A₁: To encourage him to be prompt at future meetings (lose a point if you answered something like "to tell him off" or "he had it coming").

Q₂: **What is the first step?**

A₂: To hear his explanation (maybe he left on schedule but had an automobile accident; maybe he believes the appointment was half an hour later).

Q₃: **Suppose his excuse is weak. If you were Judy how might you criticize without using the word "you"?**

A₃: Here are some possibilities: "I feel upset, Jack. I left school early to be sure to be here on time, then I have to wait 20 minutes. I feel foolish standing on the sidewalk all this time. The truth is that I've enjoyed our dates and I looked forward to being together again, but having to wait like this starts me off all wrong."

6. Two friends, X and Y, are leaving for a day on the town when X starts laughing at Y's clothing, about how his shirt doesn't match his pants, his tie is all wrong, and so on. Friend Y starts to feel annoyed.

Q₁: How can Y convey his irritation and still keep things light?

A₁: This is a good time for Y's nose to itch. Also, the "veddy fuddy" remark is appropriate, followed up, if X does not get the significance, with a telling of the joke. A friend of mine responds with "Who astya?" (Who asked you?) to unsolicited criticism. In these ways Y can express his irritation and still keep it light.

7. A young married couple describe a running argument they have been having for some time. The wife likes the house warm and sets the thermostat at 70°F. The husband insists that that is wasteful and wants the thermostat set at 65°F. The wife, who works only part-time, says that she is home a lot and is uncomfortable when it is so cold. The husband insists that she can put on a sweater. The wife calls the husband a cheapskate and a penny-pincher. The husband insists that she's just spoiled, that he works hard for his money and doesn't want to see it going up the chimney.

Q₁: What is called for here?

A₁: The problem-solving stance. First, some information is needed. What is the difference in cost between keeping the thermostat at 65°F and at 70°F? The mediator calls the local oil company and is told that if the setting were 70°F instead of 65°F all winter, the typical bill would increase about 5 percent. For this couple that would be about $100 per year.

Q₂: What suggestions might you make toward the solution?

A₂: Would they consider a compromise at, say, 68°F? How about keeping it at 70°F with the wife paying the $100 out of her salary? In fact when the wife heard the difference in cost, that is what she spontaneously volunteered to do.

Section VI

OVERVIEW

14

SUMMARY
AND CONCLUSIONS

This is a fitting point at which to take stock, to review the prescriptive principles around which this book has been written. These are:

ENGAGE PROBLEMS INTIMATELY

In material problems, appliance repair and the like, look at the object from all sides; look *into* it if possible; study parallel, properly functioning objects if available; look up reference book models if necessary. Alternative expressions of this principle are *use your eyes* (although the inner eye—visualize—is frequently intended) and *give it the time*.

Look at all problems from all angles. In mathematical problems, however, *use your eyes* also means *externalize*. Free the mind to work on the problem by relieving it of memory chores.

In problems of comprehension and remembering *use your eyes* means *visualize*. Practice having your mind light up as you read. Think of concrete examples during abstract analyses. Use imagery (such as the keyword method) when committing information to memory.

LOOK FOR SPECIAL FEATURES

Search the Problem Space. Here we function like detectives looking for clues. In mathematical puzzles these special features are frequently found in the givens or in the possible solutions of the problem.

Look at the Extremes. The solution or at least a critical component is frequently seen when the problem condition is transformed toward an extreme version. This is particularly true if some aspect of the problem approaches zero. The important role of zero was seen in the cryptarithmetic problems, the flagpole-and-rope problem, the disk-area and sphere-volume problems, as well as several others.

Look at the Simple Extreme. This is a special case of the preceding principle but is of such general value that it was given a separate chapter. In addition to the examples given in that chapter, we might note that the function-generating tables described in Chapter 3 (*externalize*) exemplify this principle.

AVOID FUNCTIONAL BLINDNESS: THINK LATERALLY

This principle articulates nicely with *use your eyes*, that is, with the prescription to look at a problem from all angles.

In addition, a variety of techniques are available to facilitate new approaches to solution. The most important of these are

Brainstorm.   Generate lots of ideas, using metaphors, random associations, even distinctly impossible arrangements if necessary.

Do not be quick to criticize.   Respect crude, even ridiculous, ideas. See first whether they can be refined.

TAKE A PROBLEM-SOLVING STANCE

This principle was presented in the context of interpersonal problem solving, where it was contrasted with emotion-dominated behavior. The principle, however, has relevance to all of problem solving. In some sense it is the *principle of intimate engagement* all over again. That principle, too, was illustrated in contrast to an inhibition, a kind of fear of taking things apart, or of becoming involved with a mathematical puzzle. In interpersonal problems, however, the problem-solving stance may be blocked by anger as well as by fear.

Specific recomendations were focused upon *brainstorming* and upon giving criticism in a sensible way, in a form likely to be effective. This included presenting yourself properly, acknowledging the other person's rights, describing the problem situation and your emotional reaction objectively (*use I-Talk*), and stressing what is positive in your relationship.

In mediating problems of others, the problem-solving stance includes *let it happen*. Faciltate the emergence of solutions by the involved parties. These have more enduring beneficial effects than do imposed solutions.

This, then, is a summary of the principles presented. An interesting final question arises in reviewing these principles. Why do they work? To put this another way, why do we humans need prescriptive principles? There appears to be a single general answer to this question: The principles help us to overcome limitations in our own human nature. These limitations fall into two categories: cognitive and emotional.

Perhaps the fundamental cognitive limitation is that the conscious mind holds only a small amount of information. This simple fact produces the benefit of externalizing and, no doubt, is at the root of einstellung. The mind, because of its limited capacity, functions best when its attention is restricted to one channel of incoming information or to one strategy. However, difficulties arise (einstellung, functional blindness) when this is the wrong channel or the wrong strategy for this particular problem. The prescriptive principles are intended to help us to be flexible, to more readily switch over.

This same limited capacity impairs our ability to commit information to memory. In this case imagery seems to function like a mind expander. We can remember more when we can "see" the information than when only the words pass through our minds. This leads to precriptions to visualize, to use imagery mnemonics.

Perhaps the most valuable recommendation for overcoming our cognitive limitations is to *simplify the problem*. Complex versions of a problem seem to dazzle the mind, to fill it to capacity just with the many details of the givens. A simple version, on the other hand, whether it is two digits (versus eight digits) in the digit-guessing problem or two disks (versus six disks) in the tower of Hanoi, gives the mind more freedom to "see" the critical relationships, to understand the problem structure. We would like, after all, not only to solve a particular problem but to understand its nature, to see what there is about the situation that gives rise to the problem. This seeing by the mind becomes more difficult the more it simultaneously must deal with a large amount of detail. Thus, *simplify the problem* says, in effect: The conscious mind has a limited capacity; eliminate, therefore, the nonessential details from the problem.

In addition to our cognitive limitations, we have emotional obstacles that must be circumvented in solving many problems. These are most obvious when the problems involve other people. Then, the various forms of anger—righteous indignation, irritation, "seeing red"—replace thought and lead us either to act foolishly or to produce unwanted side effects. Then, the various forms of fear—intimidation, anxiety, inhibition—replace thought and cause the loss of our rights. Emotional obstacles, however, are also seen in other kinds of problem solving. Some people, for example, will say that they are inhibited about taking apart a defective appliance. Others suffer from a kind of number shock and become upset when presented with any quantitative problem. Principles like *take a problem-solving stance* and *engage problems intimately* should serve to remind you that you, as a problem solver, may need to (and can) intervene with your own emotional obstacles as part of the problem-solving process.

Recognizing these limitations, cognitive and emotional, is the critical step toward improving your skills as a problem solver. The next steps along the path are to grasp and to practice the prescriptive principles for transcending these limitations. This book, it is hoped, has helped you make some progress on this path.

APPENDIX A

CHAPTER 3

p. 15:

A diagram of the rectangular board is shown in Figure A.1. From the figure we see that

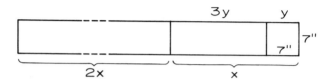

FIGURE A.1 A diagram showing the board that has been cut into three pieces. What is the area of the board?

$$y = 7 \text{ in.}$$
$$x = 4 * y = 28 \text{ in.}$$
$$\text{area} = 7 * (2 * x + x) = 588 \text{ sq. in.}$$

p. 15:

The square described in the geometry problem is shown in Figure A.2. Segment *DE* is half the length of segment *EB*. The proof is as follows:

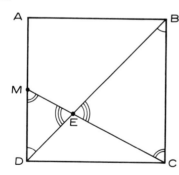

FIGURE A.2
The diagram for the geometry problem. Point *M* is the midpoint of *AD*. How does length *DE* compare with length *EB*?

1. <*DMC* = <*MCB* and <*MDB* = <*CBD* (When a line transverses a pair of parallel lines, the alternate angles are equal.)
2. <*MED* = <*BEC* (Opposite angles are equal.) Thus, triangle *MED* is similar to triangle *BEC*.
3. It is given that *MD* = (1/2)*BC*.
4. In similar triangles all pairs of corresponding sides have equal ratios.
5. Therefore, *DE* = (1/2)*EB*.

pp. 16–17:

We may use the following information to complete the matrix in Figure 3.2.

Sue is not married to Tom.
Dick is not married to Sue or to May.

Putting X's in these cells we see that Dick must be married to Bea. Putting X's in Bea's column for Tom and Harry shows that Tom must be married to May. Harry, in turn, is married to the unfaithful Sue.

p. 17:
   The matrix showing the givens is presented in Figure A.3. Use the inferences to complete the matrix. Remember, each time you put in a circle, the corresponding row and column can be filled in with X's.

	Singer	Stock-broker	Cook	Sales-man
Roger				X
Harry	X	O	X	X
George				O
Mark			X	X

FIGURE A.3
A representation of the second matrix problem, with the given information filled in.

p. 17:
   Figure A.4 shows the filled-in matrix for the three boys with their quarters and nickels. Pete and Jimmy have one and two nickels, respectively.

	Quarters	Nickels
Joey	1	3
Jimmy	3	2
Pete	5	1
Totals	9 (=$2.25)	6	Grand total = $2.55

FIGURE A.4
Completed matrix for the coin problem.

pp. 17–19:
   If, in the handshaking problem, we let H_1 be 8, that is, be the person who has shaken all eight of the others' hands, then only his

wife, W_1, can be 0, that is, can have shaken no one's hands (the others have all shaken at least the hand of H_1).

Similarly, if we let H_2 be 7 when W_2 must be 1—everyone else (except W_1) has shaken the hand of H_1 and H_2. By similar analysis H_3 is 6 and W_3 is 2, and H_4 is 5 and W_4 is 3. The anthropologist's husband, therefore, must have shaken hands 4 times.

pp. 20–21:

Suppose that, in the handball tournament, there are n contestants. Since there can be only one winner, there must be n - 1 losers. Because there is one loser per game, there must be n - 1 games.

CHAPTER 6

pp. 47–49:

The analysis in the text of the LETS + WAVE = LATER problem brought us to the point shown in the figure here:

$$
\begin{array}{ccccc}
 & 1 & E & T & 7 \\
 & 9 & 0 & V & E \\
\hline
1 & 0 & T & E & R
\end{array}
$$

In addition, we know, from column 3, that E is 1 less than T. Look, now, at column 2: T, when V is added to it, produces 1 less than itself. How can that be? It is easy if V were 9, since any number plus 9 produces a digit (in the teens) that is one less than itself. For example, 5 + 9 = 14, and so on. V, however, cannot be 9, because we have already concluded that W is 9. Suppose, however, that a (1) is carried from the first column. Then V can be 8. With that piece of information and the fact that T is 1 more than E we can turn our attention to the first column. If we let E take on different values, we immediately run into contradictions for all values but E = 5. (e.g., Can E be 4? No, because that would make R = 1, but L already = 1.) The complete solution is

$$
\begin{array}{ccccc}
L & E & T & S \\
W & A & V & E \\
\hline
L & A & T & E & R
\end{array}
\quad = \quad
\begin{array}{ccccc}
1 & 5 & 6 & 7 \\
9 & 0 & 8 & 5 \\
\hline
1 & 0 & 6 & 5 & 2
\end{array}
$$

p. 51:

Starting with Figure 6.4, we can make substantial progress in the Lonely-8 problem by focusing on PROD 2. This has the appearance of

$$\begin{array}{r} 1 \; 0 \; \text{x} \; \text{x} \\ - \; 9 \; \text{x} \; \text{x} \\ \hline 1 \; \text{x} \end{array} \longleftarrow \text{PROD} \; 2$$

We know this much about the pair of x's in the second column: They produce a difference of 1, and a (1) must be carried over to the 9 in the third column. The only pairs of digits for which these conditions can hold are 0–9, 0–8, or 1–9 (in the last two cases a (1) must be carried from the first column). Thus, PROD 2 is either 99x or 98x. This in turn means that DIV is either 123 or 124.

Two other features will lead us to the complete solution.

1. Whenever a number is carried down and the result is not larger than DIV, we place a 0 in the quotient. This happens two times—at the second and fourth quotient digit.
2. The PROD-1 subtraction pattern is identical to the PROD-2 subtraction pattern. Therefore, the first quotient digit must be an 8.

DIV, therefore, is 123 or 124, and the quotient is 80809. By multiplying each of these possible DIVs by the digits in 80809, we find that only 124 produces a result consistent with all the information. The final answer is

$$\begin{array}{r} 80809 \\ 124 \, \overline{\smash{\big)}\, 10020316} \\ \underline{992} \\ 1003 \\ \underline{992} \\ 1116 \\ \underline{1116} \end{array}$$

p. 53:
    From

$$\begin{array}{r} \text{D} \;\; \text{O} \;\; \text{N} \;\; \text{A} \;\; \text{L} \;\; \text{D} \\ + \; \text{G} \;\; \text{E} \;\; \text{R} \;\; \text{A} \;\; \text{L} \;\; \text{D} \\ \hline \text{R} \;\; \text{O} \;\; \text{B} \;\; \text{E} \;\; \text{R} \;\; \text{T} \end{array}$$

we achieved

$$\begin{array}{r} (1) \;\; (1) \quad\;\; (1) \;\; (1) \\ 5 \;\;\; \text{O} \;\;\; \text{N} \;\;\; \text{A} \;\;\; \text{L} \;\;\; 5 \\ 1 \;\;\; 9 \;\;\; 7 \;\;\; \text{A} \;\;\; \text{L} \;\;\; 5 \\ \hline 7 \;\;\; \text{O} \;\;\; \text{B} \;\;\; 9 \;\;\; 7 \;\;\; 0 \end{array}$$

We can consider the special feature that there are two A's in column 3. The only digit that, when doubled and has a (1) added can produce a 9 (or a 19) is 4 (or 9, which is excluded because E = 9). Similarly, L is either 3 or 8. Because a (1) is carried to the next column it must be 8. Continuing in this way we conclude that

$$
\begin{array}{c}
\begin{array}{l}
\text{D O N A L D} \\
\text{G E R A L D} \\ \hline
\text{R O B E R T}
\end{array}
\quad = \quad
\begin{array}{l}
5\ 2\ 6\ 4\ 8\ 5 \\
1\ 9\ 7\ 4\ 8\ 5 \\ \hline
7\ 2\ 3\ 9\ 7\ 0
\end{array}
\end{array}
$$

CHAPTER 7

pp. 56–57:

We want to prove the theorem referred to by the captain, that the area of the ring in Figure 7.2, where the length of the chord is given, is constant regardless of the radii of the circles. The ring is shown again in Figure A.5, where the radii of the two circles have been drawn in. The area of the larger circle, A_R, is

$$A_R = \pi R^2$$

and the area of the smaller circle, A_r, is

$$A_r = \pi r^2$$

The area of the disk is

$$A_{\text{disk}} = A_R - A_r = \pi R^2 - \pi r^2 = \pi(R^2 - r^2).$$

Consider now the triangle formed by R, r, and 100 in Figure A.5. By the Pythagorean theorem,

$$r^2 + 100^2 = R^2 \quad \text{or} \quad 100^2 = R^2 - r^2$$

Therefore, $A_{\text{disk}} = \pi 100^2$, regardless of the radii of the circles.

p. 58:

We treat the sphere the way we did the disk in the preceding problem. Determine the smallest sphere for which a 6-inch tube could be drilled through. This approaches a sphere whose diameter is 6 inches, for which the width of the tube approaches 0. If the volume of the resulting ring is the same for all tubes of 6-inch length, then the

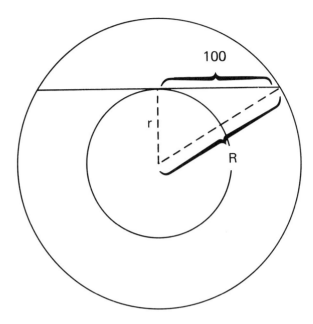

FIGURE A.5 The ring of dust with the radii of the two
circles drawn in.

ring volume is equal to the volume of a sphere 6 inches in diameter;
that is,

$$V = (\pi 6^3) / 6 = 36\pi$$

CHAPTER 8

pp. 66–67:
   We can start toward the solution of the room diagonal by noticing
that it is part of the triangle shown in Figure A.6. If we can determine
Y, the floor diagonal, then we can determine x from the Pythagorean
theorem. Of course, Y is the hypotenuse of the triangle ABY and is

$$Y^2 = A^2 + B^2$$

and

$$x^2 = Y^2 + C^2 = A^2 + B^2 + C^2$$

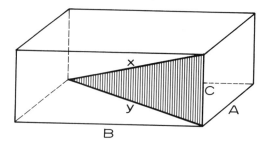

FIGURE A.6   The room showing the diagonal, x, as part of the triangle xyc.

p. 67:

Most people have trouble with this problem because they initially divide the 24 coins into two groups of coins. Take the simplest version of only 3 coins, one of which is heavy. Place a single coin in each pan, setting the third coin aside. If one pan goes down, that pan, of course, has the heavy coin. If the pans balance, then the heavy coin must, of necessity, be the coin that was set aside. Thus, you can locate a heavy coin among three in a single weighing. Follow a similar plan with 24 coins one of which is heavy. Divide them into three groups of 8, 8, and 8, placing one group on each pan and setting the third group aside. If neither side goes down then the third group must contain the heavy coin. Thus, one weighing reduces the problem into finding the heavy coin among eight. By dividing into three groups repeatedly, the heavy coin can be determined in a total of three weighings. If the nature of the defect (heavier or lighter) of the bad coin is not stipulated, then one additional weighing is required (again, try it first with three coins).

p. 67:

Take the simpler version of three stacks of three coins. Two of the stacks contain two-ounce coins, one stack is counterfeit, consisting of one-ounce coins. The bad stack may be determined in a single weighing by taking one coin from stack 1, two from stack 2, and three from 3. Place these six coins on the scale. If all the coins were good, these six coins should weigh twelve ounces. The number of ounces less than twelve gives the number of the stack with the counterfeit coins.

APPENDIX B

Answers to Exercises

INTIMATE ENGAGEMENT

6-A_2:

n	1	2	3	4
Difference between $(n + 1)^2$ and n^2	$2^2 - 1^2$ = 3	$3^2 - 2^2$ = 5	$4^2 - 3^2$ = 7	$5^2 - 4^2$ = 9

6-Q_4. $(n + 1)^2 - n^2 = n^2 + 2n + 1 - n^2 = 2n + 1$

7-A_1.

Spin, n	1	2	3	4	5	
Amount bet, A	1 2^0	2 2^1	4 2^2	8 2^3	16 2^4	$A = 2^{n-1}$

7-A_2.

Consecutive losses, C	1	2	3	4	5	6	7, win
Amount lost each spin	1	2	4	8	16	32	64
Total amount lost, T	1	3	7	15	31	63	

Notice that the amount the gambler wins the first time (i.e., on the nth spin) is 2^{n-1}. The total amount he has lost on all the preceding spins is $2^{n-1} - 1$. Thus, on spin 7 he wins $64. Up to the start of spin 7, however, he has lost $63.

10. Externalize. A picture works nicely here:

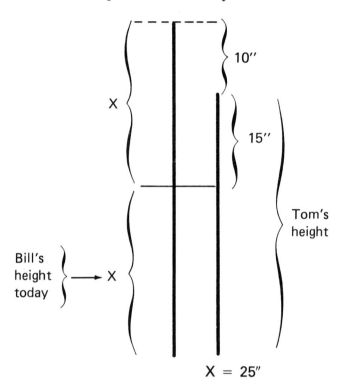

11. A picture works nicely here too:

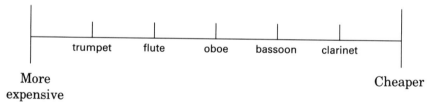

More expensive   Cheaper

SPECIAL FEATURES

2. Where on earth can a house be built such that each side has a southern exposure? The North Pole. Hence, the bear must be white.

3-A_3. In drawing a figure continuously, every time we approach an intersection we must leave it. Therefore, any point in the middle of our drawing must have an even number of lines radiating from it (in the following figure, points A, B, C, and D each have two lines). Sup-

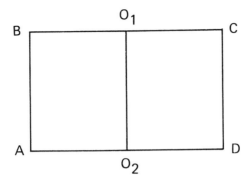

pose two points have three lines radiating, as O_1 and O_2 in the figure. The figure can still be drawn with one continuous movement, but you must start at one of these "odd" intersections and end at the other. If there are more than two odd intersections (compare the figure below) then the figure cannot be drawn in one continuous movement.

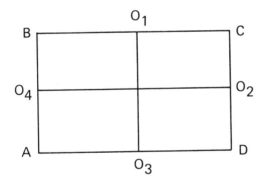

5. For any number between 1 and 999 Jean and Mary are both right. For numbers greater than 999, Jo and Mary are both right. Try zero.

6. We can establish the minimum number of moves required for any Tower-of-Hanoi problem with the aid of a function generating table. Proceed as follows:

1. We have seen that a two-disk problem requires three moves.
2. A three-disk problem (moving the disks from *A* to *C*) requires first moving the top two disks to *B* (three moves), moving the bottom disk to *C* (one move) and then the top two disks, now on *B*, to *C* (three moves). Thus, the three-disk problem is a two-disk problem followed by one move followed by another two-disk problem. It requires, therefore, $3 + 1 + 3 = 7$ moves.

3. Similarly, the four-disk problem is two three-disk problems plus one move, or 7 + 1 + 7 moves. This generates the table shown here.

NUMBER OF DISKS	MINIMUM NUMBER OF MOVES
2	3
3	3 + 3 + 1 = 7
4	7 + 7 + 1 = 15
5	15 + 15 + 1 = 31

If we study the pattern in the number of moves, we see that they are all 1 less than a power of 2; that is, the four numbers in the right-hand column may be written as $2^2 - 1$, $2^3 - 1$, $2^4 - 1$, $2^5 - 1$. In general, for n disks, the minimum number of moves required is $2^n - 1$.

7. Suppose the visitor had a five-link chain and wanted to stay five days. He need cut only the center link. He will then have three sections of 2, 1, and 2 links. He uses the single link for the first day, a two-link unit (taking back the 1) for the second day, 2 + 1 for the third, 2 + 2 for the fourth, and all of them for the fifth. Thus, one cut link will suffice for a five-link chain. Try it now for longer chains and longer visits.

8. Suppose that everything in the problem is the same except that, instead of taking a sample of size fifty, we take a sample of size two. The first child tested has an IQ of 150. Since the second child will be randomly selected, our best estimate of the second score will be something close to the mean, that is, to 100. Therefore, the mean of this sample of size two will almost always be greater than 100. This is true no matter how large the sample is, although the expected mean value comes closer to 100 as the sample is made larger.

LATERAL THINKING

3.

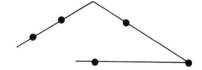

4. Beware of functional fixedness. Most people have trouble with this problem because they don't think to use the box. They see its

function as a container of matches and, therefore, fail to see other uses to which it might be put. The solution is to empty the inner box and tack it to the corkboard. The box then becomes a stand on which the candle can be safely mounted.

5. You must break out of the two-dimensional set and think in three dimensions. A pyramid, whose faces are four triangles, can be made with six matches.

6.

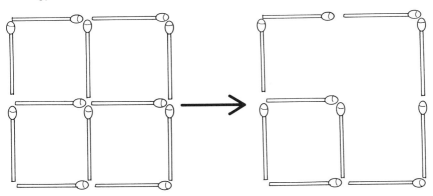

9. The fellow removed one lug from each of the other three wheels. He bolted the spare tire onto the axle with the three lugs and drove this way until he came to a station where he could buy additional lugs.

10. The driver let some air out of the tires until the truck lowered enough that he could back out.

12. The match.

13. The sun will not be shining. Thirty-six hours following noon it will be midnight.

14. All three are standing side by side in a straight line, but George is facing in the opposite direction from Bill and Mary.

15. In returning from B to A the salesman went west again. In other words, he didn't go forth and back, but went around the world.

References

ADAMS, JAMES L. *Conceptual blockbusting.* San Francisco: W. H. Freeman, 1974.

ALBERTI, ROBERT E., and MICHAEL L. EMMONS. *Your perfect right.* San Luis Obispo, Calif.: Impact Publishers, 1978.

ANDERSON, BARRY F. *The complete thinker.* Englewood Cliffs, N.J.: Prentice-Hall, 1980.

ANDERSON, RICHARD C., and JANET L. HIDDE. Imagery and sentence learning. *Journal of Educational Psychology,* 1971, *62,* 526–530.

———, and RAYMOND W. KULHAVY. Imagery and prose learning. *Journal of Educational Psychology,* 1972, *63,* 242–243.

BRANSFORD, JOHN D., and MARCIA K. JOHNSON. Contextual prerequisites for understanding: Some investigations of comprehension and recall. *Journal of Verbal Learning and Verbal Behavior,* 1972, *11,* 717–726.

BUGELSKI, B. R., EDWARD KIDD, and JOHN SEGMEN. Image as a mediator in one-trial paired-associate learning. *Journal of Experimental Psychology,* 1968, *76,* 69–73.

CHANCE, PAUL. Strategies for the Puzzled. Review of Bransford, J. D., and Stein, B. S., *The ideal problem solver,* in *Psychology Today,* April 1985, p. 72.

CHERRY, COLLIN. Some experiments on the recognition of speech with one and two ears. *Journal of the Acoustical Society of America,* 1953, *25,* 975–979.

DE BONO, EDWARD. *Lateral thinking: Creativity step by step.* New York: Harper and Row, 1970.

——— *The mechanism of mind.* New York: Simon & Schuster, 1969.

———. *PO: A device for successful thinking.* New York: Simon & Schuster, 1972.

DUNCKER, KARL. On problem solving. *Psychological Monographs,* 1945, *58* (Whole No. 270).

GARDNER, MARTIN. *Science fiction puzzle tales.* New York: C. N. Potter, 1981.

GORDON, W. J. J. *Synectics.* New York: Harper, 1961.

HAYES, JOHN R. *The complete problem solver.* Philadelphia: Franklin Institute Press, 1981.

KOHLER, WOLFGANG. *The task of Gestalt psychology.* Princeton, N.J.: Princeton University Press, 1969.

KOTOVSKY, KENNETH, JOHN R. HAYES, and HERBERT A. SIMON. Why are some problems hard? Evidence from Tower of Hanoi. *Cognitive Psychology,* 1985, *17,* 248–294.

LANGE, ARTHUR, JR., and PATRICIA JAKUBOWSKI. *Responsible assertive behavior.* Champaign, Ill.: Research Press, 1976.

LEVIN, JOEL, R. Inducing comprehension in poor readers. *Journal of Educational Psychology,* 1973, *65,* 19–24.

LEVINE, MARVIN. Hypothesis theory and nonlearning despite ideal S-R-reinforcement contingencies. *Psychological Review,* 1971, *78,* 130–140.

LUCHINS, ABRAHAM S. Mechanization in problem solving. *Psychological Monographs,* 1942, *54,* (Whole No. 6).

LUCHINS, ABRAHAM S., and EDITH H. LUCHINS. *Wertheimer's seminars revisited: Problem solving and thinking, III.* Albany, N.Y.: S.U.N.Y. at Albany, 1970.

MAIER, NORMAN R. F. Reasoning in humans, II. The solution of a problem and its appearance in consciousness. *Journal of Comparative Psychology,* 1931, *12,* 181–194.

MAYER, RICHARD E. *Thinking, problem solving, cognition.* San Francisco: W. H. Freeman, 1983.

MILLER, GEORGE A. The magical number seven, plus or minus two: Some limits on our capacity for processing information. *Psychological Review,* 1956, *63,* 81–97.

MILLER, GEORGE A., EUGENE GALANTER, and KARL H. PRIBRAM. *Plans and the structure of behavior.* New York: Henry Holt, 1960.

OSBORNE, ALEX F. *Applied imagination: Principles and procedures of creative problem solving.* New York: Scribners, 1963.

PECK, M. SCOTT. *The road less traveled.* New York: Simon & Schuster, 1978.

POLYA, GEORGE. *How to solve it.* Princeton, N.J.: Princeton University Press, 1957.

PRESSLEY, MICHAEL. Mental imagery helps eight-year-olds remember what they read. *Journal of Educational Psychology*, 1976, *68*, 355–359.

_____, JOEL R. LEVIN, and HAROLD DELANEY. The mnemonic keyword method. *Review of Educational Research*, 1982, *52*, 61–91.

RAHULA, WALPOLA. *What the Buddha taught*. New York: Grove Press, 1974.

SCRIVEN, MICHAEL. Prescriptive and descriptive approaches to problem solving. In D. T. Tuma and F. Reif (eds.), *Problem solving and education*. Hillsdale, N.J.: Erlbaum, 1980.

SWELLER, JOHN. Hypothesis salience, task difficulty, and sequential effects on problem solving. *American Journal of Psychology*, 1980a, *93*, 135–145.

_____. Transfer effects in a problem-solving context. *Quarterly Journal of Experimental Psychology*, 1980b, *32*, 233–239.

_____, and W. GEE. Einstellung, the sequence effect, and hypothesis theory. *Journal of Experimental Psychology: Human Learning and Memory*, 1978, *4*, 513–526.

TAVRIS, CAROL. *Anger: The misunderstood emotion*. New York: Simon & Schuster, 1982.

TVERSKY, AMOS, and DANIEL KAHNEMAN. Judgments under uncertainty: Heuristics and biases. *Science*, 1974, *185*, 1124–1131.

WICKELGREN, WAYNE, A. *How to solve problems*. San Francisco: W. H. Freeman, 1974.

INDEX